CHEMISTRY

For Advanced Level

Ted Lister and Janet Renshaw

Course Study Guide

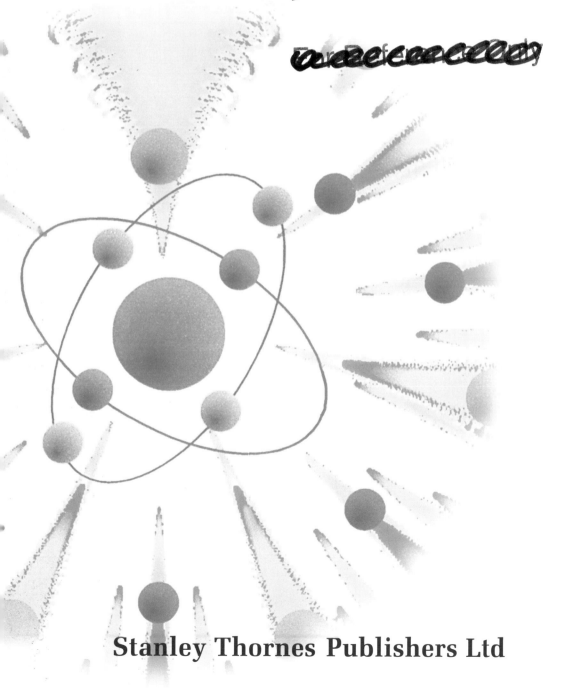

Stanley Thornes Publishers Ltd

First published in 2000 by:

Stanley Thornes (Publishers) Ltd
Ellenborough House
Wellington Street
Cheltenham
GL50 1YW

00 01 02 03 04 / 10 9 8 7 6 5 4 3 2 1

A catalogue record of this book is available from the British Library.

ISBN 0 7487 4465 7

New Understanding Chemistry for Advanced Level
ISBN 0 7487 3958 0

New Understanding Chemistry for Advanced Level plus Course Study Guide
ISBN 0 7487 4463 0

New Understanding Chemistry for Advanced Level plus Course Study Guide (Trade Edition)
ISBN 0 7487 4464 9

STRUCTURES of CHEMISTRY for Advanced Level CD-ROM
Single- and Multi-user Versions available
Free sample available on request
Please contact the publisher at the address given above
or telephone Customer Services on 01242 267273

Access to Advanced Level Chemistry
ISBN 0 7487 2334 X

Typeset by Mathematical Composition Setters Ltd, Salisbury, Wiltshire.
Printed in Great Britain by Ashford Colour Press, Gosport, Hampshire.

Contents

For Reference Only

Acknowledgements

The authors and publisher would like to thank:

The following Awarding Bodies for permission to reproduce examination questions:

The Associated Examining Board (AEB):

AQA (AEB), Stag Hill House, Guildford, Surrey GU2 5XJ
Website: www.aeb.org.uk
e-mail: aeb@aeb.org.uk

For **London** examinations:

EDEXCEL, Edexcel Foundation,
Stewart House, 32 Russell Square,
London WC1B 5DN
Website: www.edexcel.org.uk
e-mail: enquiries@edexcel.org.uk

Northern Examinations and Assessment Board (NEAB):

AQA (NEAB), Devas Street, Manchester M15 6EX
Website: www.neab.ac.uk/syllabus/maths/
chemistr.htm
e-mail: chemgeol@neab.ac.uk

Northern Ireland Council for the Curriculum Examinations and Assessment (CCEA):

CCEA, Clarendon Dock, 29 Clarendon Road,
Belfast BT1 3BG
Website: www.ccea.org.uk
e-mail: info@ccea.org.uk

For **Oxford, Cambridge** and **Oxford & Cambridge** examinations:

OCR, Publications Department,
Mill Wharf, Mill Street, Birmingham B6 4BU
Website: www.ocr.org.uk

Welsh Joint Education Committee (WJEC):

Welsh Joint Education Committee, 245 Eastern Avenue, Cardiff CF5 2YX
Website (English language): www.wjec.co.uk
         (Welsh language): www.cbac.co.uk
e-mail: bookshop@wjec.co.uk

(The Awarding Bodies bear no responsibility for the example amswers given to questions from past papers. These are the responsibility of the authors.)

Patrick McNeill for checking the accuracy of information about Advanced level and key skills qualifications.

Martyn Chillmaid for supplying the photographs on pages 4 and 11.

Introduction: Moving on from GCSE

This Course Study Guide will help you through your post-16 chemistry course. The material from GCSE that you need to be confident about is covered in the Foundations section of *New Understanding Chemistry for Advanced Level* and in more detail in *Access to Advanced Level Chemistry*. In this Course Study Guide we have concentrated on developing skills and techniques so that you can get the most out of your course and the best result possible.

The chapter 'Techniques in Advanced level chemistry' is divided into 3 sections:

- The first section talks you through some experimental work discussing the skills that you need to develop to gain maximum marks.
- The second section deals in more detail than is usual in a chemistry text with significant figures and units. These are areas of chemistry that it is useful to be confident about, but in our experience are often rather incompletely understood.
- The third section deals briefly with the use of information technology as applied to chemistry.

The following chapter on 'Key skills through Advanced level chemistry' explains why key skills are important and where to gather the evidence to prove you have the skills required from your chemistry course.

A major section of this Course Study Guide is concerned with answering examination questions on the fundamental topics of Advanced level chemistry. The chapter 'Tackling examination questions' leads you through 'specimen' answers with comments, tips and warnings of pitfalls to avoid. This helps you test your understanding and hone your examination skills. The chapter is set out as examination questions followed by suggested answers, on separate pages. You can therefore answer the question yourself and compare your answer with the one we give.

The following chapter deals with 'Synoptic assessment and questions' – questions that cover several sections of the specification (syllabus). These are an important part of A2 assessment at the end of a two-year course.

The chapter 'Revision and examination skills' contains hints and tips that we hope will help you do well in your examinations and achieve success at the end of your course.

Finally we have added a chapter that sets out and explains the Grade Criteria for all A-level chemistry specifications.

Ted Lister
Janet Renshaw

1 Techniques in Advanced level chemistry

 Practicals

Practical work

Chemistry is a practical subject, and during your Advanced level course you will need to develop your experimental skills. These will also form part of your assessment. The details of the way the assessment is carried out will vary from one Awarding Body (exam board) to another. Whatever is the means of assessment, it will cover the following areas (taken from the Subject Criteria for Chemistry):

Planning
You will need to show that you can:

- recognise and define the nature of a question or problem using available information and knowledge of chemistry;
- retrieve and evaluate information from multiple sources, including computer databases where appropriate;
- select appropriate techniques, reagents and apparatus, with due regard to precision of measurement, purity of reagents and products, safety, scale of working and the control of variables.

Implementing
You will need to show that you can:

- demonstrate the manipulative skills needed for specific chemical techniques used in the laboratory, showing a due regard for safety;
- make and record accurate observations and measurements to the degree of precision allowed by the apparatus used, including, where appropriate, logging and processing of data using information technology;
- carry out experimental work in appropriate contexts, involving:
  a) techniques of preparation and purification;
  b) qualitatitive and quantitative exercises.

Analysing evidence and drawing conclusions
You will need to show that you can:

- present work appropriately in written, graphical or other forms, using chemical nomenclature and terminology;
- interpret information gathered from experimental activities including:
  a) manipulation of data;
  b) recognition of patterns and trends in a set of data or information;
  c) identification of sources of error and recognition of the limitations of experimental measurements;

- draw valid conclusions by applying knowledge and understanding of chemistry, reporting quantitative data to an appropriate number of significant figures.

It is unlikely that any one experiment will allow you to demonstrate clearly all these skills, so you will probably find that different experiments concentrate on different areas.

The following examples should give you some idea of what the assessor is looking for in different categories.

Planning

You might be asked to do an experiment to *estimate how readily the carbonates of Group I and Group II metals decompose when heated, and relate it to the ionic radius of the metal ion.*

Firstly you will need:

- to know the products formed when these compounds decompose on heating;
- to look up the radii of the metal ions in a data book or database.

This involves **information retrieval**.

In fact the compounds decompose to produce carbon dioxide and a metal oxide according to the following equations:

Group I

$$M_2CO_3(s) \rightarrow M_2O(s) + CO_2(g)$$

Group II

$$MCO_3(s) \rightarrow MO(s) + CO_2(g)$$

where M is a Group I or Group II metal. You would need to look up these equations in a textbook to find them out (or confirm what you already knew).

You will have to decide what is meant by 'how readily the compounds decompose'. The temperature at which they begin to decompose is probably the best way to define this. This is part of **defining the problem**.

In fact most of these compounds decompose at fairly high temperatures. It is not easy in a school laboratory to measure high temperatures, so you may need to modify your thoughts. An alternative would be to heat the compounds in a Bunsen flame and time how long they took to show signs of decomposing. This is part of **selecting an appropriate technique**.

Since carbonates of Group I and II metals are colourless, there will be no colour change on decomposition, so the obvious method of deciding when they start to decompose is to look for the evolution of carbon dioxide gas. This could be done by heating the carbonates in the simple apparatus shown in Fig 1.1.

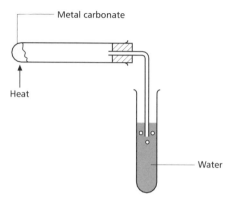

Fig 1.1 Apparatus for investigating the decomposition of carbonates

Bubbles would indicate gas given off. However, the air in the test tube would expand and give bubbles, so it would not be easy to decide just when decomposition had started.

Carbon dioxide gas turns limewater (calcium hydroxide solution) milky, so an alternative method would be to bubble the gas into limewater rather than water and look for the first signs of milkiness.

You must then decide how to make the experiment a fair test. You might decide to heat each compound at the same distance from the same Bunsen flame until you reach the same degree of milkiness, timing the procedure with a timer such as a stopwatch. You would need to use the same amount (are you going to use moles or grams?) of each compound weighed on an appropriate balance (say on a top-pan balance reading to 0.01 g). You might decide that a suitable mass to use in a test tube would be a few grams, so 1/100 mol might be suitable amount. ($M_r(CaCO_3) = 100$, so 1/100 mol = 1 g, for example.) These factors are all part of **selecting appropriate techniques, reagents and apparatus with due regard to precision of measurement, scale of working and the control of variables**.

Before starting, you would need to consider safety issues by consulting a reference source to find out about any hazards associated with the starting materials or products – **selecting appropriate techniques with due regard to safety**. For example, barium compounds are toxic and you might decide to exclude barium carbonate from the experiment for this reason. The other common Group I and II carbonates are relatively innocuous, the main hazard being the somewhat alkaline oxides which are produced on decomposition. A laboratory coat and safety glasses would be appropriate protection.

Implementing (carrying out)

You might be given an experiment to *determine the content of iron(II) sulphate in 'iron' tablets*. These tablets are taken by people whose blood is deficient in iron ions for some reason. As well as the active ingredient, iron(II) sulphate, they will contain a variety of substances to bulk out the tablet, bind the tablet together and stop the ingredients sticking to the pressing machinery.

The instructions might be:

STEP 1 Grind up two tablets with a little 1 mol dm^{-3} sulphuric acid solution in a mortar and pestle.

STEP 2 Transfer the resulting paste to a 100 cm^3 volumetric flask and make the solution to 100 cm^3.

STEP 3 Titrate 10 cm^3 portions of this solution with 0.005 mol dm^{-3} potassium manganate(VII) solution.

Your assessor would be looking for:

Weighing
- Checking that the balance is level.
- Weighing into a suitable container, such as a weighing boat, without spillage.
- Either zeroing the balance and weighing the boat before and after adding the tablets or placing the boat on the balance and taring (zeroing) the balance before adding the tablets.
- Weighing to an appropriate number of decimal places (probably to 0.01 g in the case of a top-pan balance).
- Writing down the readings immediately you have taken them.

Making up the solution (see Figure 1.2)
1. Transferring all the paste to the flask using a funnel, rinsing the weighing boat and funnel with some of the acid solution and ensuring that all the rinsings go into the flask. (Take care not to use so much solution for rinsing that you exceed the 100 cm^3 mark.)
2. Shaking to ensure that all the solid is dissolved *before* making the solution up to the 100 cm^3 mark with 1 mol dm^{-3} acid solution. (Dissolving may change the volume of liquid.)
3. Accurately filling the flask to the 100 cm^3 mark, i.e. so that the bottom of the meniscus rests on the graduation mark with the flask standing level on the bench.
4. After topping up to the mark, rocking the flask to ensure that the resulting solution is completely uniform.

Titration (see Figures 1.3 and 1.4)
- Rinsing the burette with the potassium manganate(VII) solution before use.
- Setting up the burette clamped so that it is vertical.
- Filling the burette using a funnel or small beaker and running a little of the potassium man-

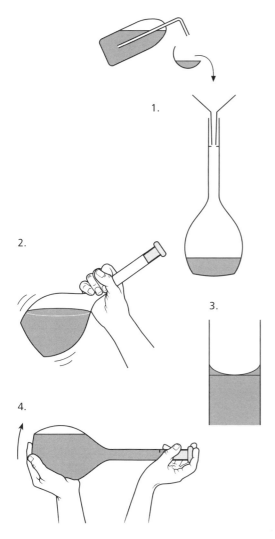

Fig 1.2 Making up a solution for a titration

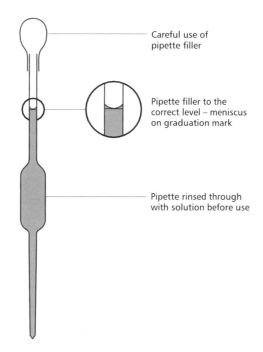

Fig 1.3 Using a pipette

ganate(VII) solution through the tap to ensure that there are no air bubbles in the tap.
- Rinsing the pipette with the iron(II) sulphate solution before use.
- Using a pipette filler to fill the pipette accurately to the mark (with the meniscus resting on the graduation mark).
- Draining the pipette into a suitably sized flask (so that it is less than half full at the end of the titration).
- Standing the titration flask on a white tile to enable the colour change to be seen clearly.
- Adding the potassium manganate(VII) solution quickly at first and then a drop at a time as the end point is approached.

This titration requires no indicator because the end point is reached when the solution in the flask just turns to the purple colour of potassium manganate(VII). You will be able to judge when the end point is approaching because the purple colour of the added potassium manganate(VII) takes longer to fade.

With a titration using an indicator that changes colour suddenly you will need first to do a rough titration adding the solution from the burette 1 cm^3 at a time until the indicator changes, to get an approximate end point.

In a titration using an indicator, the assessor will expect you to use no more than a few drops of indicator.

- Writing down the burette readings before and after the titration immediately you have taken

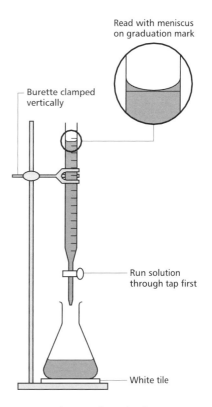

Fig 1.4 Doing a titration

them and to an appropriate number of decimal places (estimate the reading to the nearest 0.01 cm^3 if the burette is graduated in steps of 0.1 cm^3).

Readings/cm^3	1	2	3
Final	23.13	45.15	22.04
Initial	00.00	23.13	00.00
Titre	23.13	22.02	22.04

Average of 2 and 3 = 22.03 cm^3

Fig 1.5 Recording the results of a titration

- Continuing to do titrations until you have two which are within 0.1 cm^3 of each other. These two titres will be averaged for use in your calculation.

Analysing evidence and drawing conclusions

This could include processing numerical results with graphs or calculations and/or spotting patterns in observations.

For example, suppose you are given an experiment to *investigate the effect of concentration of acid on the reaction of calcium carbonate and hydrochloric acid to determine the order with respect to the concentration of hydrochloric acid*. You are asked to carry out the reaction in a flask placed on the pan of a top-pan balance and take readings of mass over a period of time. The mass will decrease as carbon dioxide gas escapes. The experiment must be repeated for different concentrations of acid.

The readings could be taken manually or (if suitable apparatus is available) the balance could be interfaced with a data logger to record the data and download it into a suitable computer package for analysis.

Your assessor would be looking for:

- Clear presentation of your results of mass and time in a suitable table which should include units, i.e. mass/g and time/minutes (or seconds). This could be done manually or by the computer.
- A graph for each concentration of acid of mass/g

Fig 1.6 Apparatus for obtaining the data in Figure 1.7

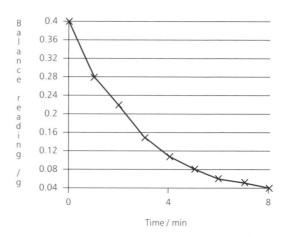

Mass against time for the reaction of CaCO₃ with HCl

Fig 1.7 A reaction rate graph produced from a spreadsheet of data

against time/minutes. This could be done manually or by the computer.
- Calculation of the slope (gradient) of each graph at time = 0. (This is the initial rate and is used because it is only at this time that we know the acid concentration *exactly*.) This could be done manually or by the computer.
- A further graph of initial rate against acid concentration. This could be done manually or by the computer.
- Calculation of the slope (gradient) of this graph. This could be done manually or by the computer.
- A statement that the slope (gradient) of this graph is 1 (within experimental error) and that this means that rate $\propto$[HCl], i.e. that the order of the reaction with respect to hydrochloric acid is 1.

Notice that it will be less work to get the computer to do the calculations and graphs but you will have to set it up and tell it what calculations to do. The assessor will also be looking for:

- A discussion of likely sources of error in the design of the experiment (systematic errors). These might include:
  - Any time lapse between starting the reaction (by dropping lumps of calcium carbonate into the acid) and starting the timing.
  - Loss of acid by 'spitting' out of the flask. This would affect the mass readings.
  - Different lumps of calcium carbonate used in different runs might have different surface areas.
- A discussion of likely sources of measurement error. These might include:
  - Timing errors, i.e. is the balance read at exactly the same time as the timer?
  - Errors in reading the balance (as the reading will be changing).
  - Making a realistic estimate of the size of the measurement errors.

Writing up practical work

Don't neglect the written side of practical work.

Here are some tips:

- Never write down your results on scraps of paper – they have a mysterious way of getting lost. Nor should you rely on your partner to write down results – he or she may be away for the next session when you need to use them.
- Write down your results with enough detail to know what they represent. You won't remember what those strange numbers mean in a week's time.
- For the same reason always write up you experiments *fully* as soon as possible after you have done them.

A useful model for writing up an experiment is to use the headings:

Title
Aim
Method
Results
Conclusion
Evaluation

although they may not all be appropriate for every experiment.

 # Units and significant figures

It is important to use the correct units in your written work and to quote numbers to an appropriate degree of precision, and examiners expect you to do so. Both these skills are fairly straightforward and well worth mastering.

Units

Ways of representing units

In everyday life we describe the speed of a car in miles per hour. The units 'miles per hour' could be written miles/hour or miles hour^{-1} where the superscript '−1' is just a way of expressing 'per' something. In science we nearly always use the metric system of units, and speed has the units metres per second, written m s^{-1}.

In each (and every) case you can think of 'per' or '/' or '$^{-1}$' as meaning 'divided by'.

Units can be surprisingly useful

A mile is a unit of distance and an hour a unit of time, so the unit 'miles **per** hour' gives you a way of remembering that speed is distance divided by time.

In the same way if you know that the units for density are 'grams **per** cubic centimetre', or g cm^{-3}, where cm^{-3} means 'per cubic centimetre', you can remember that density is mass divided by volume.

The decision makers

The scientific world now uses only **SI** units in which, for example, mass in measured in kilograms and length in metres. SI stands for **Système Internationale d'Unites**.

IUPAC (International Union of Pure and Applied Chemistry) is the international body which makes recommendations about, for example, naming chemicals. For example, they decided that element number 104 should be called rutherfordium, changed the name ethylene to ethene, and they recommend that the spelling for sulphur is sulfur and no doubt we in Britain will adopt this eventually.

Base units

The SI system is founded on seven base units and all the others can be derived from these. The base units are:

The metre, m, length
The kilogram, kg, mass
The second, s, time
The ampere, A, electric current
The kelvin, K, temperature
The mole, mol, amount of substance

which we use in Advanced level chemistry plus:

The candela, cd, luminous intensity

which we do not need to use in Advanced level chemistry.

We can present any unit we use solely in terms of base units, though we rarely need to do this. For example:

Heat energy is measured in joules, J. To work out the base units of joules we need to go back to defining energy.
Energy is force × distance and force is mass × acceleration.
Energy is therefore mass (kg) × acceleration (m s^{-2}) × distance (m). So the units are kg m^2 s^{-2} and one joule expressed in base units is 1 kg m^2 s^{-2}.

Using numbers in chemistry

Standard form

This is a way of writing very large and very small numbers in a consistent way. It makes comparison and calculations easier.

In standard form a number is written as a number multiplied by ten raised to a power. It is usual to put the decimal point to the right of the first digit of the number.

For example, 22 000 is written 2.2×10^4. 0.000 002 2 is written 2.2×10^{-6}.

You can work out the power to which ten must be raised by counting the number of places you must move the decimal point:

$$0.0005\overset{1\,2\,3\,4}{1} = 5.1 \times 10^{-4}$$

$$5\overset{4\,3\,2\,1}{1000.} = 5.1 \times 10^{4}$$

Moving the decimal point to the right gives a negative index, and to the left a postive index.

Often in calculations in chemistry, either very small or very large numbers are used. We often use prefixes as a shorthand way of expressing them. The most common prefixes, which multiply the number by a factor of 10^n are:

Prefix	nano	micro	milli	centi
Factor	10^{-9}	10^{-6}	10^{-3}	10^{-2}
Symbol	n	μ	m	c

Prefix	deci	kilo	mega
Factor	10^{-1}	10^{3}	10^{6}
Symbol	d	k	M

So 5400 m = 5.4×10^3 m = 5.4 km

Converting to base units

If you are converting from a number expressed with a prefix to one expressed in the base unit, then multiply by the conversion factor. If you have a very small or a very large number (and have to handle several zeros), the easiest way is first to convert the number to standard form (see the box 'Standard form').

A handy hint for non-mathematicians

We have found that non-mathematicians sometimes lose confidence when using small numbers, such as 0.0002. If you are not sure whether to multiply or divide then use numbers that you are happy with *because the rule will be the same.*

Here is an example:

How many moles of water in 0.0001 g? A mole of water has a mass of 18 g.
Do you divide 18 by 0.0001 or 0.0001 by 18?

If you have any doubts about how to do this then in your head change 0.0001 g to a different number, say 100 g.

How many moles of water in 100 g? A mole of water has a mass of 18 g.

Now you can see that you must divide 100 by 18. You now know that in just the same way, you must divide 0.0001 by 18.

The answer is

$$\frac{0.0001}{18} = 5.6 \times 10^{-6}$$

This idea works in any situation when you are handling small numbers.

WORKED EXAMPLE

Convert a) 2 cm, b) 100 000 000 mm to metres.

Solution
The base unit here is the metre, m.
a) $2 \text{ cm} = 2 \times \underset{\substack{\text{conversion} \\ \text{factor}}}{10^{-2}} \text{ m} = 0.02 \text{ m}$
b) $100\ 000\ 000 \text{ mm} =$
   $\underset{\substack{\text{standard} \\ \text{form}}}{1 \times 10^8} \text{ mm} = 1 \times 10^8 \times \underset{\substack{\text{multiply by} \\ \text{conversion factor}}}{\underset{\substack{\text{standard} \\ \text{form}}}{10^{-3}}} \text{ m} = 1 \times 10^5 \text{ m}$

 ## Questions

Convert to metres a) 2 000 000 nm, b) 1 500 000 μm

Using prefixes

If you want to convert a number that is expressed in a base units to one with a prefix then *divide* it by the conversion factor.

WORKED EXAMPLE

Represent 0.000 01 m in a) nanometres, b) kilometres

Solution
a) $1 \text{ nm} = 10^{-9} \text{ m}$, so the conversion factor is $\mathbf{10^{-9}}$.

   $0.000\ 01 \text{ m} = \underset{\substack{\text{standard} \\ \text{form}}}{1.0 \times 10^{-5}} \text{ m} = \underset{\substack{\text{divide by} \\ \text{conversion factor}}}{\frac{1.0 \times 10^{-5}}{\mathbf{10^{-9}}}} \text{ nm}$

   So, $0.000\ 01 \text{ m} = 1.0 \times 10^4 \text{ nm}$

Dividing by 10^{-9} is the same as multiplying by 10^9. (*Dividing* by a number expressed as 10 raised to a *negative* power is the same as *multiplying* by the number raised to the *positive* power.)

b) $1 \text{ km} = 1000 \text{ m} = 10^3 \text{ m}$, so the conversion factor is 10^3.

   $0.000\ 01 \text{ m} = 1.0 \times 10^{-5} \text{ m} = \frac{1.0 \times 10^{-5}}{10^3} \text{ km}$

Dividing by 10^3 is the same as multiplying by 10^{-3}.

So $0.000\ 01 \text{ m} = 1.0 \times 10^{-8} \text{ km}$

 ## Question

Represent:
a) 1000 m in micrometres
b) 0.001 m² in square millimetres (mm²)

Answers

a) 2×10^{-3} m   b) 1.5 m

Answers

a) $1.0 \times 10^9 \ \mu$m
b) 1.0×10^3 mm². Remember that squared units are divided twice, i.e.

$$\frac{1.0 \times 10^{-3}}{10^{-3} \times 10^{-3}}$$

Units to learn

It is a good idea to learn the units of some basic quantities by heart.

	Unit	Comment
Volume	dm^3	$1\ dm^3$ is 1 litre, L which is $1000\ cm^3$
Pressure	Pascals, $Pa = N\ m^{-2}$	
Concentration	$mol\ dm^{-3}$	
Enthalpy	$kJ\ mol^{-1}$	Occasionally $J\ mol^{-1}$ is used
Entropy	$J\ K^{-1}\ mol^{-1}$	

But remember there are no units for relative molecular mass, relative atomic mass or pH. However, we sometimes talk about the 'molar mass', i.e. the mass of one mole of substance. This *does* have units: $g\ mol^{-1}$ or $kg\ mol^{-1}$.

Don't confuse the prefix 'k' meaning 'kilo-' (which uses a lower case letter k) with the symbol 'K' for 'kelvin' (which, like all units that are derived from surnames, uses an upper case K).

 Question

How many units used in chemistry can you think of which are named after people?

Multiplying and dividing units

When you are doing calculations, units cancel and multiply just like numbers, and sometimes this can be a guide to whether you have used the right method.

WORKED EXAMPLE

The density of a liquid is $0.8\ g\ cm^{-3}$. What is the volume of a mass of $1.6\ g$ of it?

Solution

$$density = \frac{mass}{volume}$$

So $\quad volume = \frac{mass}{density}$

Putting in the values and the units:

$$volume = \frac{1.6\ g}{0.8\ g\ cm^{-3}}$$

$volume = 2.0\ cm^3$

If you had started with the wrong equation, such as

$$volume = \frac{density}{mass}$$

or volume = mass × density, you would not have obtained the correct units for volume.

Also, if you have a mathematical expression for a particular quantity then the units of the answer will be derived from those of all the quantities in the expression.

WORKED EXAMPLE

For the reaction of propanone and iodine with an acid catalyst the rate of reaction is given by the expression:

$$Rate = k[(CH_3)_2CO][H^+]$$

What are the units of k?

Solution

The rate of the reaction is measured in $mol\ dm^{-3}\ s^{-1}$ and the two concentration terms are measured in $mol\ dm^{-3}$. The units of the rate constant, k, are found from the units of the other terms, so:

$$k = \frac{Rate}{[(CH_3)_2CO][H^+]}$$

and the units are:

$$\frac{mol\ \cancel{dm^{-3}}\ s^{-1}}{\cancel{mol\ dm^{-3}}\ mol\ dm^{-3}}$$

These cancel to give the units of k as $dm^3\ mol^{-1}\ s^{-1}$.

WORKED EXAMPLE

Find the units of the equilibrium constant for the reaction:

$$N_2(g) + 3H_2(g) \rightleftharpoons 2NH_3(g)$$

Solution

$$K_c = \frac{[NH_3(g)]^2_{eqm}}{[N_2(g)]_{eqm}[H_2(g)]^3_{eqm}}$$

The units of K_c are:

$$\frac{mol^2\ dm^{-6}}{mol\ dm^{-3} \times mol^3\ dm^{-9}}$$

Cancelling the units of the terms gives: $dm^6\ mol^{-2}$

Answer

coulomb, faraday, joule, kelvin, newton, pascal, volt, ampere (amp) and there may be more. Note that when the unit is written out in full, the initial letter is lower case even though it is someone's name.

Sorting out significant figures

Many of the numbers we use in chemistry are measurements – the volume of a liquid, the mass of a solid, the temperature of a reaction vessel, for example – and no measurement can be exact. When we make a measurement, we can indicate how uncertain it is by the way we write it. For example, a length of 5.0 cm means that we have used a measuring device capable of reading to 0.1 cm, a value of 5.00 means that we have measured to the nearest 0.01 cm and so on. So the numbers 5, 5.0 and 5.00 are *different*, we say they have different numbers of **significant figures**.

What exactly is a significant figure?

In a number that has been found or worked out from measurements, the significant figures are all the digits known for certain, *plus the first uncertain one* (which may be a zero). The last figure is the uncertain one and is at the limit of the apparatus used for measuring it (see Figure 1.8).

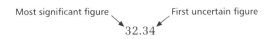

Most significant figure ↘   First uncertain figure ↙
32.34

Fig 1.8 A number with 4 significant figures

For example, if we say a substance has a mass of 4.56 grams it means that we are certain about the 4 and the 5 but not the 6 as we are approaching the limit of accuracy of our measuring device (you will have seen the last figure on a top-pan balance fluctuate). The number 4.56 has three significant figures (s.f.).

When a number contains zeros, the rules for

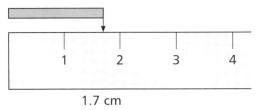

1.7 cm

This ruler gives an answer to 2 significant figures

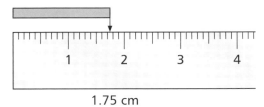

1.75 cm

This ruler gives an answer to 3 significant figures

Fig 1.9 Rulers with different precision

working out the number of significant figures are given below.

- Zeros between numbers are significant.
- Zeros to the left of the first non-zero number are not significant (even when there is a decimal point in the number).
- When a number with a decimal point ends in zeros to the right of the decimal point these zeros are significant.
- When a number with no decimal point ends in several zeros, these zeros may or may not be significant. The number of significant figures should ideally be stated. For example: 20 000 (to 3 s.f.) means that the number has been measured to the nearest 100; but 20 000 (to 4 s.f.) means that the number has been measured to the nearest 10.

The following examples should help you work out the number of significant figures in your data.

WORKED EXAMPLES

What is the number of significant figures in each of the following?

a) 11.23

Answer: 4. All non-zero digits are significant.

b) 1100

Answer: 2 (but it could be 2, 3 or 4 significant figures). The number has no decimal point so the zeros may or may not be significant. With numbers with zeros at the end it is best to state the number of significant figures.

c) 1100.0

Answer: 5. The decimal point implies a different accuracy of measurement to example (b).

d) 1.045

Answer: 4. Zeros between digits are significant.

e) 0.025

Answer: 2. Zeros to the left of the decimal point only fix the position of the decimal point. They are not significant.

Questions

How many significant figures?
a) 20 000
b) 1.030
c) 0.22
d) 22.00

Using significant figures in your answers

When doing a calculation, it is important that you don't just copy down the display of your calculator because this may have a far greater number of significant figures than the data in the question justifies. Your answer cannot be more certain than the

Answers

a) 1 (unless stated, we cannot tell whether the zeros are significant.)
b) 4 c) 2 d) 4

least certain of the information you used in working it out. So your answer should contain the same number of significant figures as the measurement which has the *smallest* number of them.

WORKED EXAMPLE

81.0 g (3 s.f.) of iron has a volume of 10.16 cm^3 (4 s.f.). What is its density?

Solution

Density = mass/volume = 81.0 g/10.16 cm^3
= 7.972 440 94 g cm^{-3} to 9 s.f.

   Since our least certain measurement was to three significant figures, our answer should not be given beyond this and we should give the density to three significant figures:

= 7.97 g cm^{-3}

If our answer had been 7.976 440 94, we would have rounded it up to 7.98 because the fourth significant figure is five or greater.

The other point to be careful about is *when* to round up. This is best left to the very end of the calculation. Don't round up as you go along because it could make a difference to your final answer.

Decimal places and significant figures

The apparatus we use usually reads to a given number of decimal places (for example hundredths or thousandths of a gram). The top-pan balances in most schools, for example, weigh to a hundredth of a gram, 0.01 g, which is to two decimal places.

   The number of significant figures of a measurement obtained by using the apparatus depends on the mass we are finding. A mass of 10.38 g has four significant figures, but a mass of 0.08 g has only one significant figure.

   By the way, calculator displays usually show numbers in standard form in a particular way. For example, the number 2.6×10^{-4} would appear as 2.6 – 04, a shorthand form which is not acceptable as a way of writing an answer. It is an error which examiners commonly complain about.

Information technology

Information technology, IT, is 'computers and the Internet' to most of us. Many people have called the 1990s the age of information technology, and IT skills are certain to be important in the next millennium in all walks of life – especially in science. So developing your IT skills will be useful in studying chemistry at Advanced level and also in whatever

career or further study you move on to. There are a number of strands to IT which are relevant to chemistry, including:

- Word processing
- Graphics
- Data logging
- Data analysis
- Spreadsheets
- Databases
- CD-ROMs
- Chemical drawing packages
- The Internet
- E-mail

As with all study and revision techniques you must use these sensibly and in the right way. Some people find IT so exciting that they get drawn into using it for its own sake and forget what they were originally trying to achieve. For example, you might find a piece of information in the index of your textbook in less time than it takes to switch on your computer and log on to the Internet to search for it.

   You don't need to have your own computer to use IT. You may be able to use one at school, the local library or even in an Internet café! And don't forget, even if you don't own or have access to a computer, you can still do well at Advanced level chemistry!

   The notes here are general ones and do not apply to any particular make or model of computer nor to any specific software package.

   The golden rule for any work you do on a computer is to make regular backups of everything you do – just in case! A 'crash' that loses all your revision notes the week before the exam would be disastrous! Back up your work onto a floppy disc or other storage device at least once a day or whenever you switch off the computer. Software is available which automatically backs up selected files at regular intervals; this is well worth considering if you use your computer a lot.

Word processing

You can use a word processor for writing up notes and laboratory reports so that they can be easily edited after checking by you or your teacher. You can add tables, charts, graphs and equations, and even pictures if you have a scanner. It is worth developing keyboard skills but with some software you can even dictate words to your computer, although they will need checking carefully for errors. All word processors come with a spell-checker but these will not know technical chemical terms. These can usually be added to the checker's dictionary as they come up. The pitfall to avoid with word processing is to spend time on presentation rather than content – patterned borders and shaded boxes will not gain you any credit.

Graphics

Graphics and drawing programs will allow you to do diagrams and paste them in your work. However, they can be time-consuming and in an exam you will still need to be able to draw diagrams by hand.

Data logging

This involves using a computer to take and store readings from an experiment. Anything that can generate a voltage can be data logged – readings from a top-pan balance, pH meter, colorimeter (see Figure 1.10) or electronic thermometer, for example. Most professional scientists will use data logging techniques routinely. Computers are especially useful for recording data over very small time intervals or very long ones – data from very fast or very slow chemical reactions are good examples. What you can use will depend on the equipment your school has. The stored data can easily be transferred into a data analysis program or a spreadsheet for further analysis or a word processing package for presentation.

Fig 1.10 Data logging using a colorimeter

Data analysis

These packages help you make sense of measurements. For example, pairs of measurements can be fed in and manipulated to find out whether there is a relationship between them. Is one proportional to the square root of the other, for example? Graphs can also be plotted with a 'least squares' analysis to produce the line of best fit. Again, you must be able to spot relationships and plot graphs manually for use in exams.

A good example of the use of a data analysis package would be to take data for the rate of a reaction at different temperatures (in °C) and plot a graph of ln (rate constant) against 1/temperature (in K) to find the activation energy (see section 26.1 in *New Understanding Chemistry for Advanced Level*).

Spreadsheets

A spreadsheet is a grid of cells that you can fill with information – words, numbers or formulae. The formulae can be used to do calculations on the numbers in the cells – for example, to add up all the numbers in a particular column or row, to square all the numbers in a row, etc. If any of the numbers in any of the cells is changed, the spreadsheet will automatically recalculate everything for you.

An example might be an investigation of an equilibrium. The equilibrium law expression can be used to calculate the concentration of one of the reactants or products if the concentrations of the others are known. A spreadsheet could be used to calculate this concentration for a variety of conditions. Figures on a spreadsheet can be plotted as graphs, charts, etc. Figure 1.11 shows the use of a spreadsheet.

Databases

These are essentially lists that you can search through in different ways. They are a searchable electronic version of file cards. You could use one to store revision notes or a revision timetable.

CD-ROMs

Many CD-ROM packages are available. They vary from general encyclopaedias such as 'Encarta' to ones on a specific topic, such as *Structures of Chemistry for Advanced Level*, a CD-ROM that can be used alongside *New Understanding Chemistry for Advanced Level*. CD-ROMs can hold text, pictures, sound clips and motion pictures. You can search for key words and links between different topics. Some even have links to sites on the Internet for further information. Text and pictures can be copied into word processing programs. But beware! You will not get any credit for simply copying chunks out of an encyclopaedia (or from the Internet) – teachers and examiners can usually spot this a mile off!

DVDs (digital versatile discs) are the successors to CD-ROMs and can hold even more information.

Chemical drawing packages

These are specific packages for producing 2D and 3D chemical structures. Most of the formulae in *New Understanding Chemistry for Advanced Level* were produced with the Chemdraw© and Chem3D© packages. 'Tools' are available to draw bonds and rings, for example, and the packages can calculate the correct bond angles and show molecules in 3D representations, which can be rotated and viewed from any angle. They are really specialised tools and it would probably not be worth buying one unless you intend to continue with chemistry beyond Advanced level. In any case you will have to learn and practise drawing chemical structures by hand for exams.

The Internet

The Internet is a means of linking computers world-wide. To access the Internet you will need a modem and a service provider and the ability to

	A	B	C	D	E	F
1	Temperature /°C	Temperature /K	Rate constant, k	1/T /K−1	log10k	
2	65	338	48700	2.958579881e−3	4.68752e+0	
3	59	332	15000	3.012048192e−3	4.176091e+0	
4	45	318	4980	3.144654088e−3	3.697229e+0	
5	35	308	1350	3.246753246e−3	3.130333e+0	
6	25	298	346	3.355704698e−3	2.539076e+0	
7	0	273	7.87	3.663003663e−3	8.9597473e−1	
8						
9						
10						
11						
12						
13						
14						
14						
15						
16						
17						
18						
19						
20						
21						
22						
23						
24						
25						

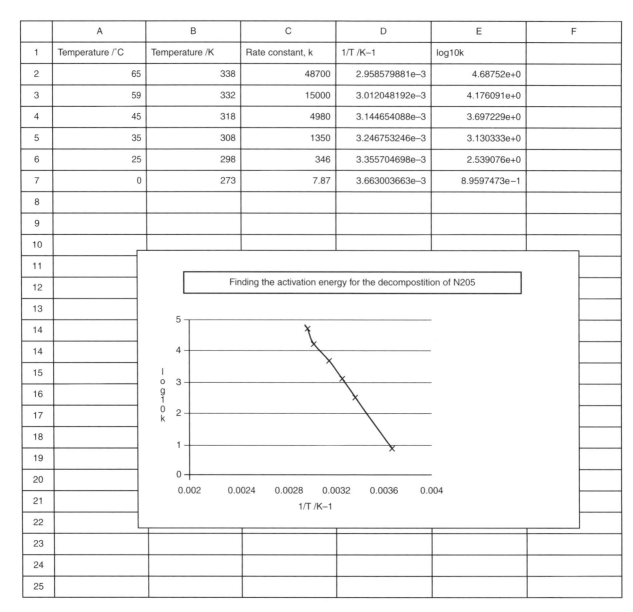

Finding the activation energy for the decompostition of N205

log10k

1/T /K−1

Fig 1.11 Using a spreadsheet to manipulate experimental results. The input data were Temperature/°C and rate constant, k. The spreadsheet has calculated 1/Temperature (in K) and $\log_{10} k$ and plotted a graph from which the activation energy can be found. Note that this particular spreadsheet uses 'e-3' to represent 10^{-3} etc. and doesn't present superscripts or subscripts. You should change them to the usual form when presenting your results

pay phone bills! The Internet can provide access to vast amounts of information but only the information people want to make available. Much of this information is accurate and useful but there is no check on any particular site. Each site has an address usually beginning 'http://www.', which you type into a program called a web browser. This will take you to the site you have chosen. Web browsers also have 'search engines' – programs that will search the world-wide web for key words. Different search engines work in different ways, so it is worth trying a few different ones.

Take care with searches both on the Internet and CD-ROMs. Too general a word (such as 'chemistry') will give you thousands of 'hits' which will be of no use. Some searching techniques can narrow down the field as shown in the example in Table 1.1. Note that search engines may vary slightly, so be familiar with the one(s) you use most.

One problem with the Internet is that it can be addictive. Take care that you don't spend a whole evening 'surfing' instead of tackling your chemistry homework

Here are some useful web addresses to start with. Many web sites have links to other similar sites.

http://www.shef.ac.uk/chemistry/web-elements/index-fr.html

This is a Periodic Table with extensive data on the elements.

http://www.anachem.umu.se/eks/pointers.htm

Example	Result
cells	Finds all articles that have the words, 'cells' or variations such as 'cell'
cell*	Finds articles that have words starting with 'cell' such as 'cellular'
cell *and* voltage	Finds articles that have the two words 'cell' *and* 'voltage'
cell *or* voltage	Finds articles that have the word 'cell' *and* articles that have the word 'voltage'
cell *not* voltage	Finds articles that have the word 'cell' but do not have the word 'voltage'
cell *near* voltage	Finds articles that have the word 'cell' within eight words of the word 'voltage'
"cell with the voltage"	Finds articles that contain the exact phrase 'cell with the voltage'

Table 1.1 Searching techniques

This also has a Periodic Table with information on reactions and Nobel prizewinners. Remember that web addresses can change and sites may cease to exist.

E-mail

This is a means of sending information – text, files, etc. – down telephone lines to other people who have computers. You will both need modems and service providers (who will give you an e-mail address). The beauty of e-mail is that the information can be copied from the e-mail and pasted into other documents or packages.

Professional scientists communicate a lot by e-mail but you might find it is most useful to contact other on-line friends to plan your social life.

2 Key skills through Advanced level chemistry

What are key skills?

Whatever you go on to do, there are certain key skills you will need as we move into the twenty-first century – in work, further education or training and everyday life.

These include:

- communication skills
- information technology skills
- application of number skills
- improving own learning and performance
- working with others
- problem solving

It is now possible to gain a qualification in these skills while you are doing your post-16 study. This qualification will be useful to show employers and provide points for entry to Higher Education. Improving your skills will also help your study.

Key skills are assessed at a number of levels. Level 3 is the one that is appropriate to post-16 students. Some of the skills can be demonstrated through activities which occur in A- or AS-level chemistry, in particular the first three skills above.

Key skills are assessed seperately from the AS/A-level through a combination of portfolio and external tests. AS/A-level chemistry can generate evidence for your skills portfolio. You should not necessarily expect to be able to demonstrate all the skills through any one subject. Below are some suggestions as to how you can develop and demonstrate key skills through the medium of chemistry.

Each key skill will lead to a separate certificate, but achievement in all the first three leads to the key skills qualification. The skills you need to demonstrate for Level 3 of this qualification are given below:

Communication Level 3

You must:

C3.1a Contribute to a group discussion about a complex subject.

Evidence must show you can:

- make clear and relevant contributions in a way that suits your purpose and situation;
- listen and respond sensitively to others, and develop points and ideas; and
- create opportunities for others to contribute when appropriate.

C3.1b Make a presentation about a complex subject using at least **one** image to illustrate the complex points.

Evidence must show you can:

- speak clearly and adapt your style of presentation to suit your purpose, subject, audience and situation;
- structure what you say so that the sequence of information and ideas may be easily followed; and
- use a range of techniques to engage the audience, including effective use of images.

Examples

You are sure to have opportunities for discussion during your course, for example about the history and development of some ideas, about the effect of some aspect of chemistry on the environment or about the economic and social aspects of chemistry.

You will need to:
- listen to what others have to say
- be sensitive to the views and feelings of others
- marshall your thoughts before you speak
- speak clearly

Your teacher will almost certainly give you the chance to make a presentation to the class. This may be about a factual topic that you have researched or a more open-ended topic such as those mentioned in C3.1a.

You will need to:
- speak clearly. It is a good idea to practise your presentation out loud to get the timing right and if you can find someone to listen to you he or she may make helpful observations about whether you can be heard, and whether your content makes sense.
- structure your arguments logically (make notes to keep yourself on track but don't just read out a prepared script). **(continued)**

You must:

(C3.1b continued)

Examples

- use one or more images. These could be posters, handouts or overhead projector transparencies, possibly prepared using a computer presentation or graphics or word processing package (thus hitting IT targets too)

These will help to keep you on track. You may base your image on a photocopied or scanned image that you have amended in some way, but whatever you do make sure it is relevant and not just decorative.

C3.2 Read and synthesise information from two extended documents about a complex subject. One of these documents should include at least one image.

Evidence must show you can:

- select and read material that contains the information you need;
- identify accurately, and compare, the lines of reasoning and main points from texts and images; and
- synthesise the key information in a form that is relevant to your purpose.

'Synthesise' means 'put together'.

This target could be approached in a number of contexts – possibly while preparing a piece of written work (essay), a talk or in planning an experiment or investigation.

You will need to:
- select relevant information from more than one source. (Use different textbooks, the Internet, etc.)
- put together relevant information in a suitable form for your purpose
- use and interpret visual information – for example a graph or diagram

Again these could be essays or plans for experiments or investigations.

C3.3 Write **two** different types of documents about complex subjects. One piece of writing should be an extended document and include at least **one** image.

Evidence must show you can:

- select and use a form and style of writing that is appropriate to your purpose and complex subject matter;
- organise relevant information clearly and coherently, using specialist vocabulary when appropriate; and
- ensure your text is legible and your spelling, grammar and punctuation are accurate, so your meaning is clear.

You will need to decide the best style for each purpose – for example practical instructions may best be presented as a series of numbered or bulleted points rather than paragraphs or prose. Diagrams or other images will almost always be needed in chemistry – especially in practical instructions.

You will need to ensure your work is legible (use a word processor if you can), accurately and correctly punctuated and spelled (use a spell-checker if possible).

Information technology Level 3

You must:

IT3.1 Plan and use different sources to search for, and select, information required for **two** different purposes.

Evidence, which must be gained in the course of a substantial activity, must show you can:

- plan how to obtain and use the information required to meet the purpose of your activity;
- choose appropriate sources and techniques for finding information and carry out effective searches; and
- make selections based on judgements of relevance and quality.

IT3.2 Explore, develop and exchange information and derive new information to meet **two** different purposes.

Evidence must show you can:

- enter and bring together information in a consistent form, using automated routines where appropriate;
- create and use appropriate structures and procedures to explore and develop information and derive new information; and
- use effective methods of exchanging information to support your purpose.

IT3.3 Present information from different sources for **two** different purposes and audiences.

Your work must include at least **one** example of text, **one** example of images and **one** example of numbers.

Evidence must show you can:

- develop the structure and content of your presentation using the views of others, where appropriate, to guide refinements;
- present information effectively, using a format and style that suits your purpose and audience; and
- ensure your work is accurate and makes sense.

Examples

Your purpose could be preparing for a discussion, preparing a talk, writing an essay, planning practical work.

Sources could include:
- general CD-ROMs such as *Encarta* or other encyclopaedias; specialist chemistry CD-ROMs such as *Structures of Chemistry for Advanced Level* or *The Chemistry Set*. Find out what is available in your school library.
- the Internet. A few ideas for sites are given on page 12 or you can use a search engine (see Chapter 1). All sorts of things are available including Periodic Table databases of elements, mass/infra-red/NMR spectra, and data about compounds. There is so much information that you will need to restrict your searching. Remember also some sites will be more reliable than others. – one run by a university chemistry department or the Royal Society of Chemistry is more likely to be accurate than an unknown site. One run by a chemical company is less likely to stress pollution problems while the Friends of the Earth site may highlight them. You need to exercise judgement! See the tips for searching in Chapter 1, page 12.

This could include the use of a spreadsheet or other data handling package to process the results of some experimental work.

If your school has an intranet, you could share your results with the rest of your group using e-mail.

You could produce a practical write-up using a word processor. Your report could include diagrams from a graphics package, results which have been processed using a spreadsheet and charts or graphs drawn from the data in the spreadsheet.

Application of number Level 3

You must:

N3.1 Plan, and interpret information from **two** different types of sources, including a large data set.

Evidence, which must be gained in the course of a substantial and complex activity, must show you can:

- plan how to obtain and use the information required to meet the purpose of your activity;
- obtain the relevant information; and
- choose appropriate methods for obtaining the results you need to justify your choice.

N3.2 Carry out multi-stage calculations to do with:

a amounts and sizes;
b scales and proportion;
c handling statistics;
d rearranging and using formulae.

You should work with a large data set on at least **one** occasion.

Evidence must show you can:

- carry out calculations to appropriate levels of accuracy, clearly showing your methods; and
- check methods and results to help ensure errors are found and corrected.

N3.3 Interpret results of your calculations, present your findings and justify your methods. You must use at least **one** graph, **one** chart and **one** diagram.

Evidence must show you can:

- select appropriate methods of presentation and justify your choice;
- present you findings effectively; and explain how the results of your calculations relate to the purpose of your activity.

Examples

This could relate to the planning of practical work and treatment and calculation of results – using paper and pencil, calculator or computer (for example a spreadsheet). If you take results from the whole of your teaching group you could assemble a large data set. Also you could compare your results, obtained from a small number of cases, with a database of other people's results, for example a Periodic Table or database of information about compounds. You could compare your own results for, say, $\Delta H_f^\ominus$ for two or three alcohols with those of the rest of the class to give a bigger data set and with accepted results from a data book or database to give an even bigger one.

You will certainly find plenty of opportunities for these skills when dealing with your practical results. Most quantitative work will involve rearranging formulae, scaling and proportion and amounts and sizes. Calculating averages (of your results and those of the whole group) could give you a start at least on statistics, as would the plotting of graphs with lines or curves of best fit.

Many of your practical write-ups, especially those that involve making measurements, will allow you to demonstrate these skills. For example, an investigation of reaction rates at different temperatures might involve plotting a graph of, say, volume against time, calculating the gradient of this graph to give the rate and then plotting a second graph – ln (rate) against $1/T$ – whose gradient allows you to calculate E_A.

3 Tackling examination questions

Introduction

In this chapter we go over a number of past examination questions on the topics in Part B: Fundamentals from *New Understanding Chemistry for Advanced Level*. We have talked around the answers, putting the chemistry in context, pointing out common mistakes and pitfalls and also what examiners are looking for. As far as is possible in a book, we have tried to do this as though we were sitting down with you as a student, discussing issues that arise from each question.

Inevitably the *detail* of examination questions changes from one Awarding Body to another, and as specifications change. We have selected the examples here to include core content and to illustrate the principles of answering examination questions.

Of course what you need to know is just what to write on the exam paper to get full marks, so we draw a distinction between this and our commentary by printing the commentary in the right-hand column. Remember that your answers need not be exactly the same as ours (they may even be better) but the meaning should be the same.

Take any relative atomic masses you need from the Periodic Table at the end of this book.

The Questions

1 This question is about atomic structure, electron arrangements and ionisation energies.

Potassium was discovered and named in 1807 by the British chemist Sir Humphry Davy. The mass spectrum of a sample of potassium is shown below:

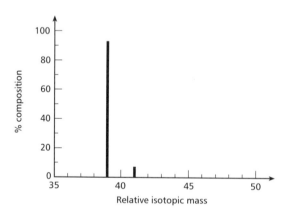

(a) (i) Use this mass spectrum to estimate the percentage composition of potassium isotopes in the sample.
Copy and complete the table below to show the percentage composition and atomic structure of each potassium isotope.

Isotope	Percentage composition	Protons	Neutrons	Electrons
^{39}K				
^{41}K				

(ii) The relative atomic mass of the potassium sample can be determined from its mass spectrum.
Explain what you understand by the term *relative atomic mass*.

(iii) Calculate the relative atomic mass of the potassium sample. [7]

(b) Complete the electronic configuration of a potassium atom. $1s^2$ [1]

(c) The first and second ionisation energies of potassium are shown in the table below.

Ionisation	1st	2nd
Ionisation energy/kJ mol^{-1}	419	3051

(i) Explain what you understand by the term *first ionisation energy* of potassium.

(ii) Why is there a large difference between the first and the second ionisation energy of potassium?

[5]

[O & C 1997, specimen]

Answer

Comments

a) (i)

Isotope	Percentage composition	Protons	Neutrons	Electrons
^{39}K	93%	19	20	19
^{41}K	7%	19	22	19

All isotopes of potassium have 19 protons and 19 electrons – only the number of neutrons varies. So they have the same electron arrangement and therefore behave identically chemically.

(ii) The relative atomic mass is the mass of an atom relative to the mass of an atom of ^{12}C on a scale on which the mass of an atom of carbon is *exactly* 12.000.

The relative atomic mass is the weighted average of the masses of all the isotopes. Only carbon has an atomic mass that is *exactly* a whole number.

(iii) 100 atoms of potassium would consist of 93 of ^{39}K and 7 of ^{41}K, so the average mass would be

$$\frac{(93 \times 39) + (7 \times 41)}{100} = 39.14$$

The relative atomic mass, A_r, is a number without units.

b) $(1s^2)2s^2\, 2p^6\, 3s^2\, 3p^6 3s^1$

Notice how this corresponds to the simpler notation (2,)8,8,1. Also, as a check, potassium is in Group I, so your arrangement must end up with one electron in an outer s shell.

c) (i) The energy that must be put in to remove completely the outer electrons from one mole of isolated gaseous potassium atoms to give a mole of isolated gaseous potassium ions, K^+.

i.e. ΔH for the process $K(g) \longrightarrow K^+(g) + e^-$

The easiest way to describe this is to refer to the equation – the state symbols are important.

(ii) The first electron is removed from the outer shell. It is relatively far from the nucleus and 'feels' a shielded nuclear charge of $19 - (2 + 8 + 8) = 1$. The second electron comes from the next shell in. It is nearer the nucleus and 'feels' a shielded nuclear charge of $19 - (2 + 8) = 9$. So on two counts it is more strongly held.

The large jump between the first and second ionisation energies is why potassium normally forms ions with one positive charge.

2 This question is about enthalpy changes, bond enthalpies (bond energies) and Hess's law.

a) In $\Delta H^{\ominus}$, what does the symbol $^{\ominus}$ indicate? [1]

b) Some mean bond enthalpies are given below.

Bond	C—C	H—H	Cl—Cl	C—H
Mean bond enthalpy/kJ mol^{-1}	348	436	242	412

(i) Write the equation for the reaction used to define the bond enthaply of a chlorine–chlorine bond. Include state symbols.

(ii) Why is the term *mean bond enthalpy* used in the table instead of just *bond enthalpy*?

(iii) Use the data above to predict what happens first when a sample of propane, C_3H_8, is cracked in the absence of air and explain your prediction. [5]

c) Use the following data to calculate the standard enthalpy of formation of propane.

$C_3H_8(g) + 5O_2(g) \rightarrow 3CO_2(g) + 4H_2O(l)$ $\quad \Delta H^{\ominus} = -2220$ kJ mol^{-1}

$H_2(g) + \frac{1}{2}O_2(g) \rightarrow H_2O(l)$ $\quad \Delta H^{\ominus} = -286$ kJ mol^{-1}

$C(s) + O_2(g) \rightarrow CO_2(g)$ $\quad \Delta H^{\ominus} = -394$ kJ mol^{-1} [4]

[NEAB 1998]

Answer

a) The symbol indicates that the heat energy is measured under standard conditions, i.e. at a temperature of 298 K and a pressure of 100 kPa (standard atmospheric pressure). The concentration of any solution present is 1 mol dm^{-3}.

b) (i) $Cl_2(g) \rightarrow 2Cl \cdot (g)$

   (ii) Mean bond enthalpy is used because the enthalpy of bonds such as C—C and C—H varies in different compounds. The tabulated value is an average or mean value taken over several compounds.

   iii) *Prediction*: A C—C bond will break rather than a C—H bond.
       Explanation: The C—C bond is weaker than the C—H bond.

c)

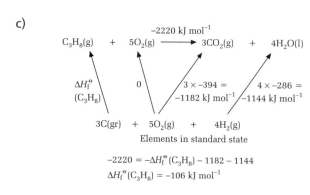

$$-2220 = -\Delta H_f^{\ominus}(C_3H_8) - 1182 - 1144$$
$$\Delta H_f^{\ominus}(C_3H_8) = -106 \text{ kJ mol}^{-1}$$

Comments

Heat energy measured under these conditions is called enthalpy.

The dot indicates that the chlorine atoms each have an unpaired electron.

There is only one value for Cl—Cl and H—H bonds because these bonds exist only in Cl_2 and H_2.

Remember the bond enthalpy is the enthalpy which has to be *put in* to break bonds.

$\Delta H_f^{\ominus}$ of $O_2(g)$ is zero – don't forget that all elements in their standard states have $\Delta H_f^{\ominus}$ of zero by definition. This question is about Hess's law which states that the enthalpy change for a chemical reaction is the same irrespective of the route by which it occurs – in this case either directly or via the elements.

Changing the direction of the formation of propane step reverses the sign of the enthalpy change.

3 This question is about Born–Haber cycles – the enthalpy changes which occur when an ionic compound is formed from its elements.

(a) (i) Using data provided, construct a Born–Haber cycle for magnesium chloride, $MgCl_2$, and from it determine the electron affinity of chlorine.

	$\Delta H/\text{kJ mol}^{-1}$
Enthalpy of atomisation of chlorine	+122
Enthalpy of atomisation of magnesium	+148
First ionisation energy of magnesium	+738
Second ionisation energy of magnesium	+1451
Lattice enthalpy of magnesium chloride	−2526
Enthalpy of formation of magnesium chloride	−641

[5]

(ii) The theoretically calculated value for the lattice enthalpy of magnesium chloride is 2326 kJ mol^{-1}. Explain the difference between the theoretically calculated value and the experimental value given in the data in (a)(i), in terms of the bonding of magnesium chloride. [3]

[London (Nuffield) 1998, part]

Answer

a) i)

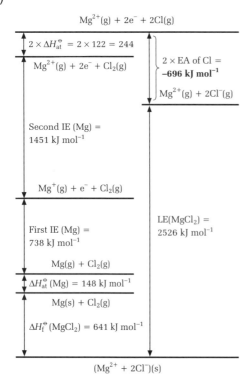

$Mg^{2+}(g) + 2e^- + 2Cl(g)$

$2 \times \Delta H_{at}^{\ominus} = 2 \times 122 = 244$

$2 \times EA$ of $Cl = $
-696 kJ mol^{-1}

$Mg^{2+}(g) + 2e^- + Cl_2(g)$

$Mg^{2+}(g) + 2Cl^-(g)$

Second IE (Mg) =
1451 kJ mol^{-1}

$Mg^+(g) + e^- + Cl_2(g)$

First IE (Mg) =
738 kJ mol^{-1}

LE(MgCl$_2$) =
2526 kJ mol^{-1}

$Mg(g) + Cl_2(g)$

$\Delta H_{at}^{\ominus}$ (Mg) = 148 kJ mol^{-1}

$Mg(s) + Cl_2(g)$

$\Delta H_f^{\ominus}$ (MgCl$_2$) = 641 kJ mol^{-1}

$(Mg^{2+} + 2Cl^-)(s)$

$2 \times EA$ of $Cl = 696$ kJ mol^{-1}
so EA of $Cl = 348$ kJ mol^{-1}

ii) In all ionic compounds, there is some degree of covalent bonding caused by the positive ion distorting the electron cloud of the negative ion. This is called polarisation.

Comments

- Since there are two chlorine atoms involved on this cycle, it includes $2 \times$ electron affinity of chlorine.
- Since Mg forms Mg^{2+} ions we use the *sum* of the first two ionisation energies for Mg, *not* $2 \times$ first ionisation energy:

1st IE(Mg) is ΔH for $Mg(g) \rightarrow Mg^+(g) + e^-$
2nd IE(Mg) is ΔH for $Mg^+(g) \rightarrow Mg^{2+}(g) + e^-$

not $Mg(g) \rightarrow Mg^{2+}(g) + 2e^-$

The electron affinity of two atoms of chlorine is found from the rest of the figures. It is
$(641 + 148 + 738 + 1451 + 244) - 2526 = 696$

Fajans' rules state that polarisation is greater for:

- small highly charged positive ions (cations)
- large highly charged negative ions (anions)

4 This question is about intermolecular forces – van der Waals forces, dipole–dipole forces and hydrogen bonding.

The boiling points of four compounds which have hydrogen bonds between their molecules are shown below:

Compound	Formula	Molar mass /g mol^{-1}	Boiling point /°C
Water	H_2O	18	100
Methanol	CH_3OH	32	65
Ethanol	C_2H_5OH	46	79
Butan-1-ol	C_4H_9OH	74	117

(a) Draw a diagram showing the position of a hydrogen bond between two molecules of methanol.

[1]

(b) By considering the structures and intermolecular forces involved, explain:

   (i)   why water has a higher boiling point than ethanol. [2]

   (ii) why methanol has a lower boiling point than ethanol. [2]

(c) Butan-1-ol has an isomer named ethoxyethane, $C_2H_5OC_2H_5$.

   Explain why there are no hydrogen bonds between ethoxyethane molecules. [1]

(d) Iodine is almost insoluble in water but is more soluble in ethoxyethane.

   (i)   What type of force is present between molecules of iodine in a crystal? [1]

   (ii) Explain why iodine is more soluble in ethoxyethane than in water. [3]

[London (Nuffield) 1997]

Answer

a)

b) i) Water forms more hydrogen bonds than ethanol. A water molecule has two hydrogen atoms bonded to the oxygen and two lone pairs on the oxygen atom and therefore on average can form *two* hydrogen bonds per molecule. Ethanol has two lone pairs on the oxygen but only one hydrogen atom bonded to the oxygen and can therefore on average form only one hydrogen bond per molecule.

ii) Methanol and ethanol have comparable amounts of hydrogen bonding, but methanol has weaker van der Waals forces between its molecules than ethanol because it is smaller (by a —CH_2— group). It therefore has a lower boiling point than ethanol.

c) None of the hydrogen atoms in an ethoxyethane molecule is bonded to an electronegative atom.

d) i) van der Waals forces

ii) This is an example of the 'like dissolves like' rule. Iodine molecules and ethoxyethane molecules both bond via van der Waals forces and these same forces hold the two molecules together in the mixture. So, very little change occurs when iodine and ethoxyethane mix.
   Water molecules are held together by strong hydrogen bonds. These require more energy to be broken than do van der Waals forces. A comparable amount of energy is not given out on mixing iodine and water because these molecules can only bond together with van der Waals forces. So iodine is not very soluble in water.

Comments

Hydrogen bonds are formed *only* between a hydrogen atom that is covalently bonded to a highly electronegative atom (nitrogen, oxygen or fluorine) and a highly electronegative atom (nitrogen, oxygen or fluorine).
   The O—H⋯O system is linear because the two pairs of electrons repel one another as far away as possible.

The C_2H_5— hydrogens *cannot* participate in hydrogen bonding because they are not bonded to an electronegative atom.

van der Waals forces depend on the number of electrons and hence the size of the molecule (i.e. they are roughly proportional to its relative molecular mass).

5 This question is about equilibria and the equilibrium law expression.

Each of the equations **A**, **B**, **C** and **D** represents a dynamic equilibrium.

A $N_2(g) + O_2(g) \rightleftharpoons 2NO(g)$ $\Delta H^{\ominus} = +180 \text{ kJ mol}^{-1}$
B $N_2O_4(g) \rightleftharpoons 2NO_2(g)$ $\Delta H^{\ominus} = +58 \text{ kJ mol}^{-1}$
C $3H_2(g) + N_2(g) \rightleftharpoons 2NH_3(g)$ $\Delta H^{\ominus} = -92 \text{ kJ mol}^{-1}$
D $H_2(g) + I_2(g) \rightleftharpoons 2HI(g)$ $\Delta H^{\ominus} = +180 \text{ kJ mol}^{-1}$

(a) Explain what is meant by the term *dynamic equilibrium*.   [1]

(b) Explain why a catalyst does not alter the position of any equilibrium reaction.   [2]

(c) The units of the equilibrium constant K_c, for one of the above reactions are mol dm^{-3}. Identify the reaction **A**, **B**, **C** or **D** which has these units for K_c and write the expression for K_c for this reaction.   [2]

(d) The graphs below show how the yield of product varies with pressure for three of the reactions **A**, **B**, **C** and **D** given above.

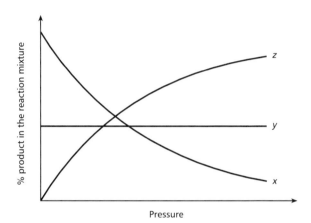

(i)   Identify a reaction from **A**, **B**, **C** and **D** which would have the relationship between yield and pressure shown in graphs *x*, *y* and *z*.

(ii) Explain why an industrial chemist would not use a very low pressure for the reaction represented in graph *x*.

(iii) Explain why an industrial chemist may not use a very high pressure for the reaction represented in graph *z*.

(iv) Add to the above graphs a line to show how the product yield would vary with pressure if the reaction which follows curve *z* was carried out at a temperature higher than that of the original graph.   [7]

[NEAB 1998]

Answer

a) Both forward and back reactions continue at the same rate, so there is no change in the composition of the reaction mixture.

b) A catalyst affects the rate of both forward and back reactions equally.

c) *Reaction*: **B**

$$K_c = \frac{[NO_2(g)]_{eqm}^{\,2}}{[N_2O_4(g)]_{eqm}}$$

d) i)   *Graph x*: **B**
        Graph y: **A** or **D**
        Graph z: **C**

  ii)   The rate of reaction would be too slow.

 iii)   High pressure requires a strong and therefore expensive plant even though the yield would be large.

 iv)

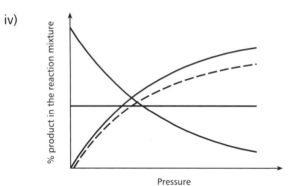

Comments

All chemical equilbria are dynamic.

Catalysts work by reducing the activation energy of a reaction, which applies equally to both forward and back reactions.

The units cancel $\dfrac{\cancel{mol\,dm}^{-3} \times mol\,dm^{-3}}{\cancel{mol\,dm}^{-3}}$

K_c for reactions A and D have no units, K_c for C has the units $dm^6\,mol^{-2}$.

Check that you can do these.

These are examples of Le Châtelier's principle. Increasing the pressure will move the equilibrium in the direction that produces fewer molecules, which tends to reduce the pressure. Reactions A and D have the same number of molecules on both sides and are therefore unaffected by pressure.

Though the yield would be high.

Reaction C is exothermic. According to Le Châtelier's principle, increasing the temperature will decrease the yield at all pressures.

6 This question is about the pH scale and strong and weak acids.

A lake in Scotland had a pH of 4.2.

(a) State the relationship between pH and hydrogen ion concentration. [1]

(b) Calculate the hydrogen ion concentration of the lake in Scotland. [1]

(c) Explain, using suitable examples and equations, the difference between a strong acid and a weak acid. [3]

[Oxford 1997]

Answer

a) $pH = -\log_{10}[H^+(aq)]$

b) $4.2 = -\log_{10}[H^+(aq)]$
$\log_{10}[H^+(aq)] = -4.2$
$[H^+(aq)] = 6.31 \times 10^{-5}$ mol dm^{-3}
$\qquad = 6.3 \times 10^{-5}$ mol dm^{-3} (to 2 s.f.)

c) Strong acids are fully dissociated into ions in solution when dissolved in water, for example, hydrochloric acid:

$HCl(aq) \rightarrow H^+(aq) + Cl^-(aq)$

Weak acids are partially dissociated, for example, ethanoic acid:

$CH_3CO_2H(aq) \rightleftharpoons CH_3CO_2^-(aq) + H^+(aq)$

Comments

Remember the square brackets represent concentration in mol dm^{-3}.

Use the inverse log function on your calculator. Do not copy the calculator display in the form 6.31 –05.

Only about four of every 1000 ethanoic acid molecules are dissociated in a solution of concentration 1 mol dm^{-3}.

7 This question is about oxidation numbers (oxidation states).

The stoichiometric equation for the catalytic oxidation of ammonia in an industrial process is:

$$4NH_3 + 5O_2 \rightarrow 4NO + 6H_2O$$

Name which elements here undergo a change in oxidation state and give the initial and final oxidation states.

(WJEC 1996)

Answer

Name of element	Oxidation state	
	Initial	Final
nitrogen oxygen	–III 0	+II –II

Comments

You need to remember the rules for working out oxidation numbers. The relevant ones are:

- Hydrogen is always +I in compounds except with Groups I and II.
- Uncombined elements (oxygen in this case) are always zero.
- Oxygen is always –II in compounds except in peroxides and superoxides, and compounds with fluorine.
- The sum of all the oxidation numbers in a neutral compound is zero.

As a check, the total increase in oxidation numbers must equal the total decrease. Here, each of the four nitrogen atoms goes up five (total increase 20) and each of the ten oxygen atoms goes down by two (total decrease 20).

8 This question is about reaction rates and order of reactions.

The data below refer to the reaction

$$X + Y \longrightarrow products$$

Concentration of X/mol dm^{-3}	Concentration of Y/mol dm^{-3}	Rate/mol dm^{-3} s^{-1}
0.01	0.01	1.0×10^{-4}
0.01	0.02	2.0×10^{-4}
0.02	0.02	2.0×10^{-4}

Deduce the overall order of the reaction. [1]

[WJEC 1997]

Answer

The overall order of the reaction is 1.

Comments

Compare the first two rows of figures. [Y] doubles while [X] is unchanged. The rate doubles, so the reaction is first order with respect to Y.

Look at the second and third rows of figures. [X] doubles while [Y] is unchanged. The rate is unchanged. This means the reaction is zero order with respect to X.

The overall order is the sum of the orders with respect to all the reactants:

Rate = $k[Y]^1[X]^0$, so the overall order is 1.

9 This question is about trends in atomic radii in the Periodic Table. These are related to the number of protons in the nucleus of each atom and the electron arrangement.

The atomic radii of elements in groups 1–7 of the Periodic Table are shown in the Table below. Some radii have been omitted.

		Group						
		1	**2**	**3**	**4**	**5**	**6**	**7**
Period 2	element	Li	Be	B	C	N	O	F
	atomic radius/nm	0.134	0.125	0.090	0.077	0.075	0.073	0.071
Period 3	element	Na	Mg	Al	Si	P	S	Cl
	atomic radius/nm	0.154	0.145	0.130	0.118	0.110		0.099
Period 4	element	K	Ca	Ga	Ge	As	Se	Br
	atomic radius/nm	0.196	0.174		0.122	0.122	0.117	0.114

(a) (i) State the trend shown in atomic radius across a period.

(ii) Explain this trend. [3]

(b) (i) State the trend shown in atomic radius down a group

(ii) Explain this trend. [2]

(c) Mendeleev studied periodic data to make predictions for the properties of elements yet to be discovered.

Use the data above to predict the atomic radius of

(i) S

(ii) Ga [2]

[O & C 1997, specimen]

Answer

a) i) The atomic radius decreases.

   ii) As we cross a period, the nuclear charge increases. This attracts the outer electrons closer to the nucleus.

b) i) The atomic radius increases
   ii) Each step down a group means that the atom has an extra shell of electrons.

c) i) Sulphur: 0.105 nm (to 3 s.f.)
   ii) Gallium: 0.148 nm

Comments

The nucleus is about 10^4 times smaller than the atom, so the extra protons and neutrons in the nucleus do not affect the size of the atom.

For sulphur take the average of the radii of the elements either side.

$$\frac{0.110 + 0.099}{2} = 0.1045 \text{ nm}$$

$$= 0.105 \text{ nm (to 3 s.f. – the same as in the data)}$$

For gallium take the average of the radii of the atoms on either side.

$$\frac{0.174 + 0.122}{2} = 0.148 \text{ nm}$$

10 This question asks for an explanation of ionisation energies and has mole calculations on the reactions of acids.

The plot below is of the logarithm of successive ionisation energies (I.E.) for all the electrons in a gaseous potassium atom.

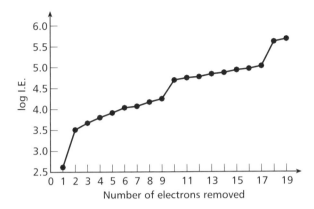

(a) Explain why

   (i) the first ionisation energy has such a low value, [1]

   (ii) the plot shows a general increase in the values of these ionisation energies. [1]

(b) (i) Give a reason for the change in ionisation energies between the 1st and 2nd ionisations. [1]

   (ii) Name the orbital from which the 10th electron is removed. [1]

(c) State why the 18th and 19th ionisations are so high. [1]

(d) Describe by means of a sketch, or otherwise, how the graph for calcium would differ from that for potassium. [1]

(e) A small piece of pure calcium metal was allowed to react with a large volume of water. It was found that 50 cm^3 of aqueous hydrochloric acid of concentration 0.2 mol dm^{-3} had to be added to the mixture to produce a neutral solution.

   (i) Write a balanced equation for the reaction between calcium and water. [1]

   (ii) Calculate the mass of calcium used. [2]

   (iii) State the volume of the same hydrochloric acid which would have been required if the same number of moles of pure sodium had been used in place of the calcium. Explain your answer. [2]

[WJEC 1997]

Answer

a) i) The first electron is relatively easy to remove. It is being removed from the outer shell, so it is far from the nucleus and 'feels' a shielded nuclear charge of one unit.

ii) The greater the positive charge on the ion, the more difficult it is to remove the electron. The first electron is being removed from a neutral atom, the second from a K^+ ion and the third from K^{2+} and so on.

b) i) There is a large jump between the first and second ionisation energies because the second electron to be removed comes from a shell closer to the nucleus than the first, and feels a shielded nuclear charge of 9+ rather than 1+.

ii) 2p

c) The two electrons come from the orbital closest to the nucleus and 'feel' the full unshielded nuclear charge.

d)

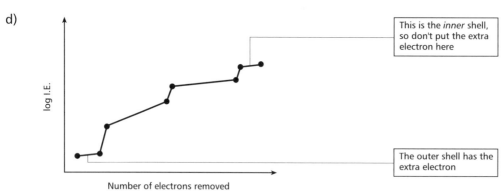

Calcium has *two* electrons in the outer shell, which are relatively easy to remove.

e) i) $Ca(s) + 2H_2O(l) \rightarrow Ca(OH)_2(aq) + H_2(aq)$

Comments

The electron arrangement of potassium:

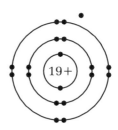

The outer electron feels a positive charge of $19 - (2 + 8 + 8) = 1$.

Remember that the first ionisation energy refers to:

$K(g) \rightarrow K^+(g) + e^-$

and the second ionisation energy refers to:

$K^+(g) \rightarrow K^{2+}(g) + e^-$

and not:

$K(g) \rightarrow K^{2+}(g) + 2e^-$

The electron configuration is $1s^2 2s^2 2p^6 3s^2 3p^6 4s^1$. Electrons are removed starting from 4s, and moving inwards.

An electron in shell 3 'feels' a shielded nuclear charge of $19 - (2 + 8) = 9+$.

Don't forget the state symbols. Notice that the question asks for the reaction of calcium and *water*, not the reaction between the product and hydrochloric acid.

ii) $Ca(OH)_2(aq) + 2HCl(aq) \rightarrow CaCl_2(aq)$
   1 mol   2 mol $+ 2H_2O(l)$

number of moles of acid $= \dfrac{M \times V}{1000} = \dfrac{0.2 \times 50}{1000}$

$$= 1 \times 10^{-2}$$

no. moles $Ca(OH)_2 = \frac{1}{2}$ no. moles HCl

$$= 0.5 \times 10^{-2}$$

This equals no. of moles of Ca (from first equation)

A_r for Ca $= 40$,

So mass of Ca $= 40 \times 0.5 \times 10^{-2}$

$$= 0.2 \text{ g}$$

iii) 25 cm^3 of hydrochloric acid. Sodium would have produced sodium hydroxide with water and this reacts in the ratio 1 : 1 with hydrochloric acid. Therefore only half the volume of acid would be needed.

In this question (as in all questions about titrations) always write an equation for the relevant reaction.

To find the number of moles in any solution use the equation

$$\dfrac{M \times V}{1000}$$

where M is the concentration in mol dm^{-3} and V the volume of the solution in cm^3.

$Na(s) + 2H_2O(l) \rightarrow NaOH(aq) + \frac{1}{2}H_2(aq)$
$NaOH(aq) + HCl(aq) \rightarrow NaCl(aq) + H_2O(l)$
1 mol   1 mol

11 This question is about the reaction of halogens. It also asks you to make some predictions about an everyday situation which you are not expected to have covered in your course.

A bottle of bleach bears the slogan 'Contains sodium hypochlorite. This decays into common salt and water after it has killed germs... Do not use with lavatory cleaners containing acid'.

(a) Some lavatory cleaners contain hydrochloric acid.

    (i) Hydrochloric acid is a solution of hydrogen chloride, HCl, in water.
       Write the equation *including state symbols* for the reaction of HCl gas with water.   [2]

    (ii) Explain how this shows that hydrogen chloride is behaving as an acid.

    (iii) Hydrochloric acid reacts with sodium hypochlorite to give chlorine gas and sodium chloride.   [2]
       Write an equation for this reaction. Sodium hypochlorite has the formula NaClO.   [2]

    (iv) State why the instructions say 'Do not use with lavatory cleaners containing acid'.   [2]

(b) On standing (or on warming), a solution of sodium hypochlorite decomposes as follows:

$$2NaClO \rightarrow 2NaCl + O_2$$

    (i) Write oxidation states under all the chemical symbols in this equation.   [3]

    (ii) Is the label on the bottle accurate about what happens to the sodium hypochlorite?   [1]
       Explain your answer.   [1]

(c) The concentration of sodium hypochlorite in a bleach can be measured by warming the solution and measuring the volume of oxygen collected.

    $100 \ cm^3$ of a bleach solution gave $24 \ cm^3$ of oxygen when warmed. Calculate the mass of NaClO in $1.0 \ dm^3$ of the bleach.
    (A_r: Na = 23; O = 16; Cl = 35.5; 1.0 mol of oxygen molecules occupies $24 \ dm^3$ under the condition of the experiment.)   [4]

(d) Another method for determining the concentration of bleach is to add an excess of potassium iodide solution and titrate the liberated iodine with sodium thiosulphate solution. The solution goes colourless when all the iodine has reacted with sodium thiosulphate.

    (i) What colour is a solution of iodine in water?   [1]

    (ii) Describe how you would proceed to determine accurately the volume of sodium thiosulphate solution needed to react with a certain amount of iodine in solution. Assume you have available several flasks containing equal amounts of iodine in solution and a burette containing sodium thiosulphate solution.   [4]

[O & C Salters 1997]

Answer

a) i) $HCl(g) + H_2O(l) \rightarrow H_3O^+(aq) + Cl^-(aq)$

 ii) It is donating a proton (H^+ ion) to water.

 iii) $2HCl(aq) + NaClO(aq) \rightarrow NaCl(aq)$
$+ H_2O(l) + Cl_2(g)$

 iv) Chlorine, a harmful gas is produced.

b) i) $2NaClO \rightarrow 2NaCl + O_2$
${\scriptstyle +I\ +I\ -II}{\scriptstyle +I\ -I}\ \ {\scriptstyle 0}$

 ii) No
Oxygen, not water, is formed.

c) 24 cm^3 O$_2$ is the volume of

$$\frac{24}{24\,000} = \frac{1}{1000} \text{ mol } O_2$$

From the equation, this is produced by

$$\frac{2}{1000} \text{ mol NaClO.}$$

1.0 dm^3 of bleach (1000 cm^3) contains $\dfrac{2}{100}$ mol NaClO.

So, 100 cm^3 of bleach contains $\dfrac{2}{1000}$ mol NaClO.

M_r NaClO is $23 + 35.5 + 16 = 74.5$

So $\dfrac{2}{100}$ mol NaClO has a mass of

$$\frac{2}{100} \times 74.5 = 1.49 \text{ g.}$$

1 dm^3 of bleach contains 1.5 g NaClO to 2 s.f..

d) i) Brown

 ii) Note the volume reading of the burette containing the sodium thiosulphate solution. Gradually add this solution from the burette to the iodine solution in the flask until the iodine solution becomes a pale yellow colour. Add a few drops of starch solution to the flask (which gives a blue-black complex). Now add sodium thiosulphate solution a drop at a time until the blue-black colour in the flask just disappears. Note the volume reading of the burette. Repeat the whole procedure with fresh flasks of iodine until two readings of the volume of sodium thiosulphate needed agree within 0.1 cm^3.

Comments

Don't forget the state symbols.

The Lowry–Brønsted theory of acidity states that acids are proton donors. An H^+ ion is a bare proton. H_2O is able to accept a proton because it has lone pairs of electrons.

Again, don't forget the state symbols.

Chlorine was used as a poison gas in World War I.

Sodium always forms the +I oxidation state in is compounds. Oxygen forms the –II oxidation state in all its compounds except in peroxides and superoxides and compounds with fluorine. The oxidation state of an uncombined element is *always* zero.

Sodium chloride is common salt.

Show as much of your working as you can, so that if you make a simple arithmetical error you will lose very few marks.

Read the question carefully. You are asked for the mass in 1.0 dm^3 of bleach, not 100 cm^3.

Give your answer to two significant figures because this is the number to which the *least* certain quantity is given.

12 This question is about isomerism in organic chemistry.

(a) Explain what is meant by the term *stereoisomerism*. [1]

(b) Draw three-dimensional representations of each of the four stereoisomers of structural formula **A**.

$$CH_3CH(OH)CH\!\!=\!\!CHCH_3$$

A

Number the structures you have drawn 1 to 4. [4]

(c) With reference to the structures you have drawn, or using other examples of your own choice, explain the meaning of, and structural requirements for:

(i) optical isomerism; [2]

(ii) *cis*- and *trans*-isomers. [2]

(d) State which of the compounds 1–4 in part (b) will have the same boiling points, explaining the reason for your choice. [2]

[Oxford 1997]

Answer

a) Molecules which have the same molecular formula and the same functional groups but whose atoms have different spatial arrangements are stereoisomers.

b)

CH₃–C=C structure, labelled 1, with CH₃, H, H, CH₃, C*, H, OH

CH₃–C=C structure, labelled 2, with CH₃, H, CH₃, H, C, H, OH

CH₃–C=C structure, labelled 3, with CH₃, H, H, CH₃, C, HO, H

CH₃–C=C structure, labelled 4, with CH₃, H, CH₃, H, C, HO, H

c) i) This involves a pair of non-identical mirror image isomers. A carbon atom attached to four different groups is required such as the one marked with a star in the answer in b).

   ii) Two groups on the same side of a double bond are *cis*- and two on opposite sides are *trans*-. 1 and 3 above are *cis*-; 2 and 4 are *trans*-.

d) 1 and 3 will have the same boiling points. 2 and 4 will have the same boiling points (but different from 1 and 2). (1 and 3) and (2 and 4) are both pairs of optical isomers which will have identical properties (except for their effect on polarised light).

Comments

The chiral carbon (*) is the same in any of the isomers. The most obvious type of isomerism in this molecule is *cis–trans-*, which is about the arrangement of groups around the double bond.

In rough, first draw the *cis-* and *trans-* isomers. You will then see that there is also a carbon atom, which has four different groups attached to it and is therefore chiral.

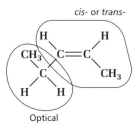

cis- or *trans-*

Optical

This carbon and its attached groups will exist as a pair of non-identical mirror images. You *must* draw the arrangement of groups around the chiral carbon using three-dimensional representation. Optical isomers *cannot* be distinguished by flat representations.

The isomers are called enantiomers. They rotate the plane of polarisation of polarised light in different directions but otherwise have identical physical properties.

13 This question is about alkanes – their shapes and isomerism.

Butane, C_4H_{10}, can be used as a fuel. Here are some data about butane:
Boiling point, 0 °C;
Standard enthalpy change of combustion, $\Delta H_{c,298}^{\ominus} = -2880$ kJ mol^{-1}.

(a) To what homologous series does butane belong? [1]

(b) Butane has one structural isomer.

    (i) Say what you understand by the term *structural isomer*. [2]

    (ii) Draw the full structural formula of the structural isomer of butane and name it. [2]

(c) All the H—C—H bonds in butane have the same angle in the three-dimensional molecule.
State, and explain, the value of this angle. [3]

(d) 'The standard enthalpy change of combustion of the isomer in part (b) will be very similar to that of butane itself as all the bonds are the same.'
Say whether or not this statement is correct and explain why. [3]

O & C (Salters) 1997, part specimen]

Answer

a) The alkanes

b) i) Structural isomers have the same molecular formula but their atoms are bonded together differently. They may have different functional groups or different branching of their carbon chains.

ii)

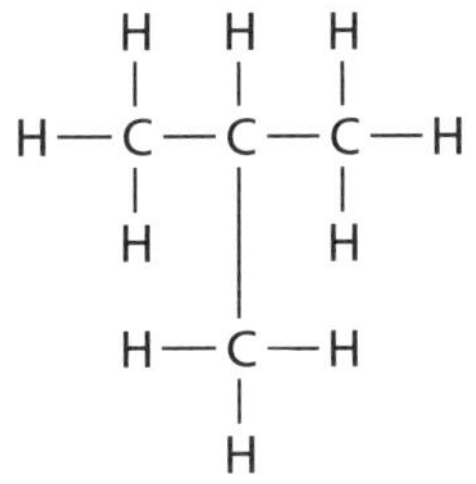

```
        H   H   H
        |   |   |
    H — C — C — C — H
        |   |   |
        H   |   H
            |
        H — C — H
            |
            H
```

Name: methylpropane

c) 109.5°. This is the tetrahedral angle. Each carbon atom has four identical electron pairs in its outer shell. These repel one another to get as far apart as possible.

d) Yes it is. Both butane and methylpropane have 10 C—H bonds and 3 C—C bonds. The same bonds have approximately the same energy in different molecules.

Comments

Homologous series are families of organic compounds with the same functional group. Each member differs from the next by a $-CH_2-$ group.

Contrast this with stereoisomers in question 12.

Butane and methylpropane are chain branching isomers. The name is based on propane because the longest unbranched chain has three carbon atoms.

Bond energies of the same bond are not *exactly* the same in different molecules.

14 This question is about alkenes – their isomers and their reactions.

(a) Give the structural formulae of the four isomeric alkenes of molecular formula C_4H_8. [4]

(b) Name the only branched C_4H_8 isomer and outline a mechanism to show how this molecule is protonated by sulphuric acid. [3]

(c) Give the structure and name of the organic product obtained when the reaction mixture in part (b) is poured into an excess of water. [2]

[NEAB 1998]

Answer

a)

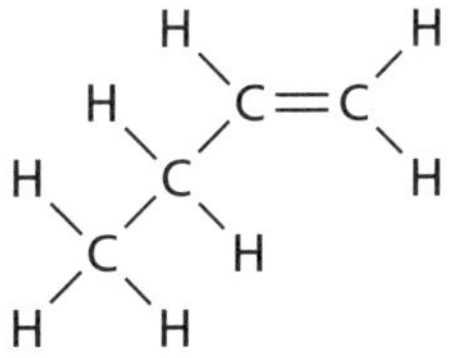

Isomer 1

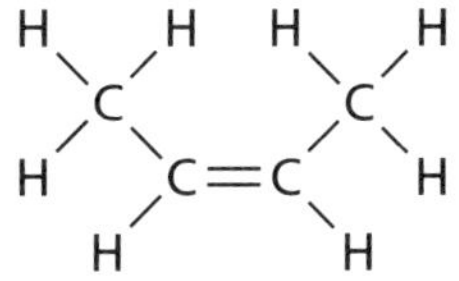

Isomer 2

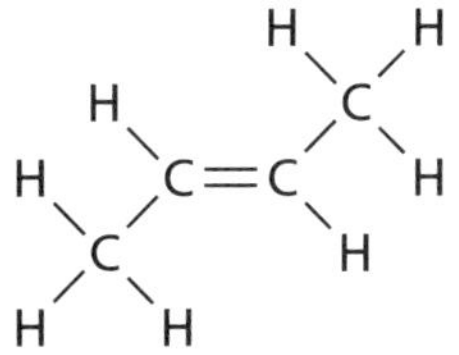

Isomer 3

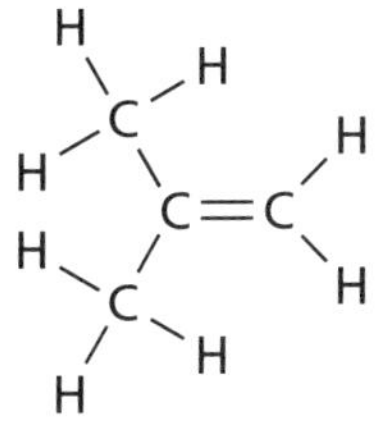

Isomer 4

b) *Name of branched isomer:* methylpropene
(Isomer 4 above)
Mechanism:

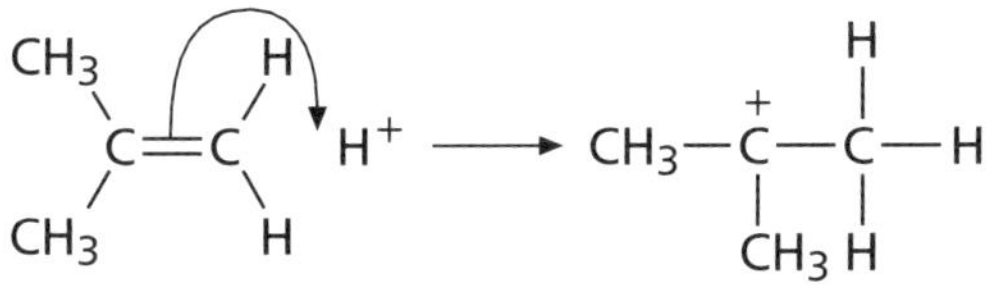

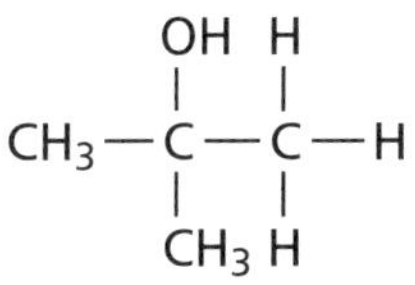

c) *Structure:*

Name: 2-methylpropan-2-ol

Comments

You could draw the

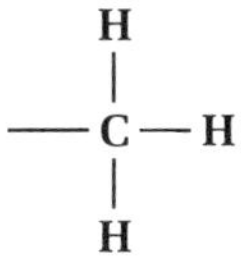

group as $-CH_3$ because a displayed formula (which shows every atom and every bond) is not asked for. In this context do not draw the molecules as being linear, such as

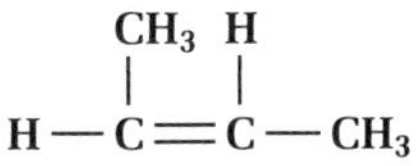

because *cis-* and *trans-* isomers (2 and 3) cannot be distinguished. This is a common error.

The positive charge ends up on the carbon with the two $-CH_3$ groups, as the inductive (electron releasing) effect of these groups stabilises the charge. This is the basis of Markovnikov's rule. The inductive effect is sometimes drawn $\rightarrow CH_3$.

15 This question is about haloalkanes – their isomerism and their substitution and elimination reactions

(a) The graphical formulae of **two** of the **four** structureal isomers of C_4H_9Br are:

Isomer 1   Isomer 2

   (i) Draw the graphical formulae of the other **two** structural isomers. [2]

   (ii) Which **one** of these four isomers reacts most readily with aqueous sodium hydroxide? [1]

(b) When **Isomer 1** reacts with aqueous sodium hydroxide, a reaction takes place in which the molecule is attacked by the hydroxide ion.

$$C_4H_9Br + NaOH \rightarrow C_4H_9OH + NaBr$$

   (i) What feature of the C_4H_9Br molecule makes it liable to attack by the hydroxide ion? [1]

   (ii) Give the name of the type of mechanism in this reaction. [2]

(c) When **Isomer 2** reacts with sodium hydroxide in an alcohol solvent, a reaction represented by the following equation takes place.

$$C_4H_9Br + NaOH \rightarrow C_4H_8 + NaBr + H_2O$$

   (i) State the type of reaction taking place. [1]

   (ii) Draw graphical formulae to show **two** of the isomers of C_4H_8 which are formed in this reaction. [2]

(d) A compound **Y** has the composition by mass $C = 29.76\%$, $H = 4.18\%$, $Br = 66.6\%$ and a relative molecular mass of 241.90.

   (i) Calculate the molecular formula of **Y**. [3]

   (ii) **Y** is formed in an addition reaction between an alkene and bromine. Draw the structural formula of the alkene. [1]

[AEB 1995]

Answer

Comments

a) i)

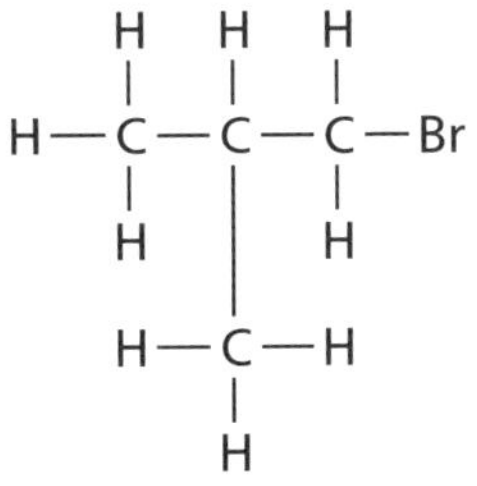

H—C—C—C—Br with structure (Isomer 3):

```
        H   H   H
        |   |   |
    H—C—C—C—Br
        |   |   |
        H   |   H
            |
        H—C—H
            |
            H
```
Isomer 3

```
        H   Br  H
        |   |   |
    H—C—C—C—H
        |   |   |
        H   |   H
            |
        H—C—H
            |
            H
```
Isomer 4

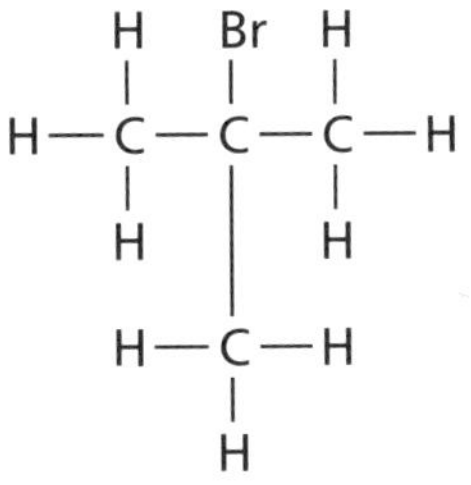

ii) Isomer 4

b) i) The C—Br bond is polarised $C^{\delta+}—Br^{\delta-}$.

ii) Nucleophilic substitution

c) i) Elimination

ii)

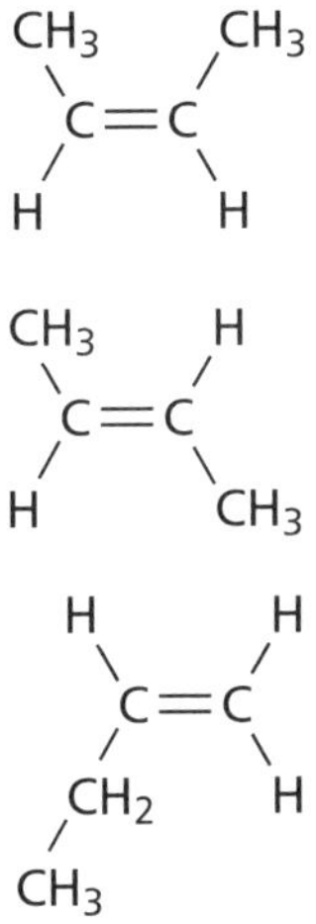

```
    CH3     CH3
      \     /
       C = C
      /     \
    H         H
```

```
    CH3     H
      \     /
       C = C
      /     \
    H         CH3
```

```
     H       H
      \      /
       C = C
      /      \
    CH2        H
    /
  CH3
```

```
        H   H   H   Br
        |   |   |   |
    H—C—C—C—C—H
        |   |   |   |
        H   H   H   H
```

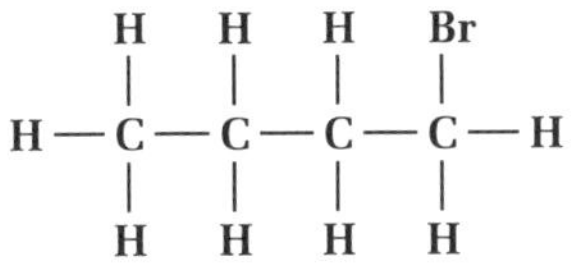

'Graphical' formula means the same as 'displayed' formula. All the atoms and bonds are drawn separately. The structure above is the same molecule as Isomer 1, differing only in that the right-hand C—C bond has rotated. It is therefore not a different isomer.

This is a tertiary haloalkane. Loss of Br^- produces a carbocation in which the positive charge is stabilised by the inductive (electron-releasing effect) of the three $CH_3—$ groups.

The OH^- ion will attack the $C^{\delta+}$.

A nucleophile is a reagent that attacks $C^{\delta+}$. The reaction is a substitution because a Br atom has been *replaced* by an OH group.

A molecule (HBr) is lost from the C_4H_9Br.

Any two of these will do.

d) In 100 g **Y**:

$$\text{moles of C} = \frac{29.76}{12} = 2.48,$$

$$\text{moles of Br} = \frac{66.06}{80} = 0.826,$$

$$\text{moles of H} = \frac{4.18}{1} = 4.18$$

Ratio C : Br : H

$$\frac{2.48}{0.826} : \frac{0.826}{0.826} : \frac{4.18}{0.826}$$
$$3 : 1 : 5$$

Divide the number of moles of each element by the smallest number of moles to get a whole number ratio.

The empirical formula is therefore C_3H_5Br, $M_r = (3 \times 12) + (5 \times 1) + 80 = 121$
The M_r of the compound is 241.90, twice as large, so its molecular formula is $C_6H_{10}Br_2$.

The empirical formula is the simplest whole number ratio of the atoms in the compound. The molecular formula is the actual numbers of atoms of each element in a molecule of the compound. The molecular formula is always a whole number multiple of the empirical formula. The multiple (2 in this case) is found by dividing M_r of the molecule by M_r of the empirical formula.

ii)

Before addition of the Br_2, the alkene's molecular formula must have been C_6H_{10}. The alkene must have a ring because otherwise it has two hydrogen atoms too few. (The formula of a chain alkene with 6 carbon atoms is C_6H_{12}). Always look out for a ring when short of hydrogens in the empirical formula.

Other isomers with smaller rings and side chains are possible.

16 This question is about the reactions of primary, secondary and tertiary alcohols – especially oxidation and dehydration.

(a) Write an equation for the oxidation of pentan-2-ol by acidified potassium dichromate(VI) showing clearly the structure of the organic product. You may use the symbol [O] for the oxidising agent. [2]

(b) Pent-2-ene can be formed by the dehydration of pentan-2-ol. Give the reagent and conditions used. Outline a mechanism for this reaction. [6]

(c) Alcohols **E**, **F** and **G** are branched-chain isomers of pentanol.
E cannot be oxidised by acidified potassium dichromate(VI).
F can be oxidised by acidified potassium dichromate(VI) but cannot be dehydrated.
G can be oxidised by acidified potassium dichromate(VI) and can also be dehydrated.
Draw a possible structure for each of the three alcohols. [3]

(d) Draw and name the isomer of pentene which has three peaks in its low-resolution proton NMR spectrum and give the relative areas under the peaks. [4]

[NEAB 1998]

Answer

a)

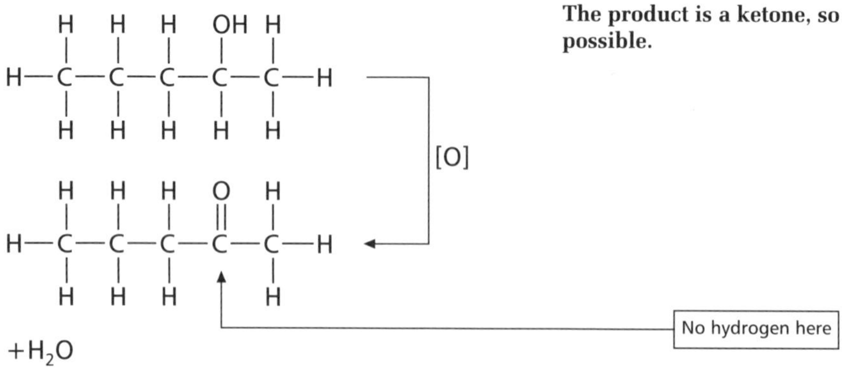

$+H_2O$

b) *Reagent*: concentrated sulphuric acid
Conditions: excess acid

Mechanism:

c) E

Comments

The product is a ketone, so no further oxidation is possible.

No hydrogen here

It is a common mistake to add a hydrogen to a $C=O$ carbon atom in ketones.

With excess alcohol an ether is formed.

Alcohols can also be dehydrated by passing their hot vapours over a catalyst such as aluminium oxide or phosphorus pentoxide.

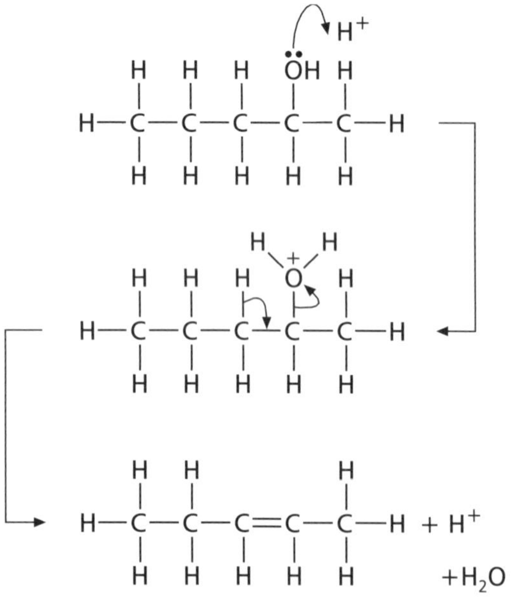

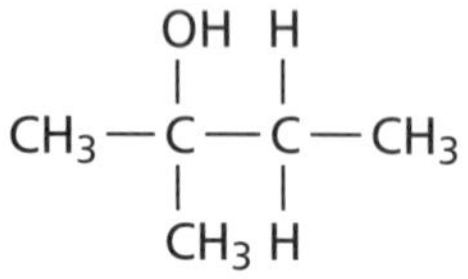

This is a tertiary alcohol and therefore cannot easily be oxidised. It can be dehydrated because there are carbons bearing hydrogen atoms next to the —OH group as shown:

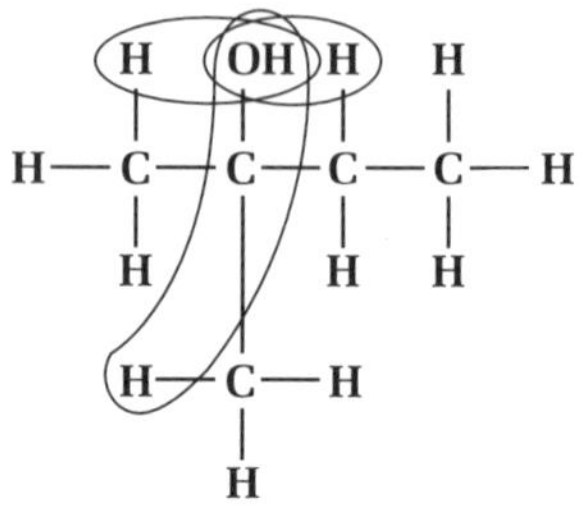

F

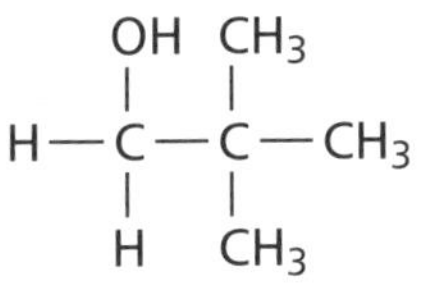

$$\begin{array}{ccc} OH & CH_3 & \\ | & | & \\ H-C-C&-CH_3 \\ | & | & \\ H & CH_3 & \end{array}$$

This is a primary alcohol and therefore can be oxidised. The carbon next to that with the —OH group has no hydrogen and the molecule cannot therefore be dehydrated.

G

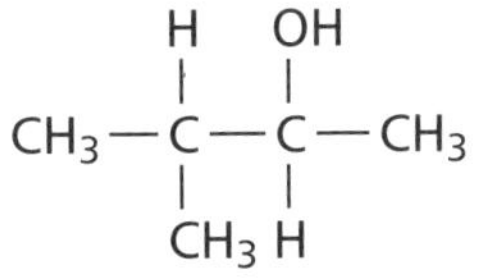

$$\begin{array}{ccc} H & OH & \\ | & | & \\ CH_3-C-C&-CH_3 \\ | & | & \\ CH_3 & H & \end{array}$$

This is a secondary alcohol and therefore can be oxidised (to a ketone). It can be dehydrated because there are carbon atoms bearing hydrogen atoms next to the —OH group as shown:

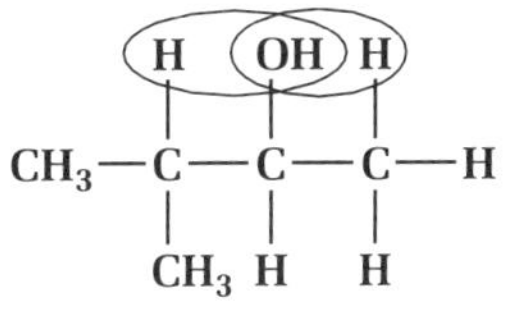

$$\begin{array}{cccc} H & OH & H & \\ | & | & | & \\ CH_3-C-C-C&-H \\ | & | & | & \\ CH_3 & H & H & \end{array}$$

Pent-2-ene in fact has *cis*- and *trans*- isomers. Both would have similar low-resolution NMR spectra.

d)

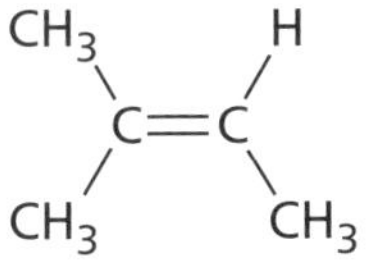

$$\begin{array}{cc} CH_3 & H \\ \diagdown & \diagup \\ C=C \\ \diagup & \diagdown \\ CH_3 & CH_3 \end{array}$$

Name: 2-methylbut-2-ene
Relative areas: 6 : 1 : 3

The hydrogen atoms in the two —CH$_3$ groups on the left are in similar environments and give a single peak of area 6 units. The hydrogen atom of the CH group gives a peak of area 1 unit and those of the —CH$_3$ group on the right give a peak of area 3 units.

4 Synoptic assessment and questions

Introduction

As well as tackling questions that focus on particular topics you will also have to tackle so-called synoptic questions. In examiner's jargon, these involve 'drawing together knowledge, understanding and skills learned in different parts of your course'. This may make it difficult for you to choose which question or questions to tackle (if you have a choice).

The best advice is not to rush your decision. There will probably be parts of several questions that you can do and parts that are not quite up your street. Look at the marks for each part and from these roughly work out the question you are most likely to obtain the most marks for.

We have selected some questions, each of which has a theme, and analysed them to show the topics they cover. The chapter references are to *New Understanding Chemistry for Advanced Level*.

The Questions

1 The theme of this question is copper.

It tests:

- your ability to work out electron arrangements of atoms and ions (Chapters 2 and 7)
- your ability to calculate oxidation numbers (Chapter 13)
- your ability to do simple calculations on compositions of compounds (Chapter 4)

- your common-sense appreciation of environmental problems
- thermochemical cycles (Chapter 8)
- hydration and hydration enthalpies (energies) (Chapter 10)
- lattice enthalpies (Chapter 9)

Many copper minerals are found in hydrothermal deposits where they were formed by crystallisation from very hot solutions. Deep underground the conditions are like a giant pressure cooker and water is still liquid at high temperatures. Under these conditions, minerals that are regarded as 'insoluble' in the laboratory can dissolve. When the solutions cool the minerals crystallise out.

a) One such copper mineral is chalcopyrite, $CuFeS_2$, which contains both copper and iron in the +2 oxidation state. The mineral is smelted in modern works by heating with air:

$$4CuFeS_2 + 10.5O_2 \rightarrow 4Cu + 2FeO + Fe_2O_3 + 8SO_2$$

(i) Write the electron configurations, in terms of s, p and d electrons for:

a copper atom; [1]
a Cu^{2+} ion. [1]

(ii) Copper is reduced in this reaction. Complete a copy of the chart below to show two elements that are **oxidised** in the reaction.

element		from	to
copper	reduced	+2	0
....	oxidised	......	......
....	oxidised	......	......	[1]

(iii) Calculate the percentage of copper by mass in a sample of rock containing 0.50% by mass of chalcopyrite, assuming this is the only source of copper in the rock.
(Relative atomic masses: $A_r(Cu) = 64$, $A_r(Fe) = 56$, $A_r(S) = 32$) [3]

(iv) Suggest an environmental problem which arises as a result of your answer to (iii). [2]

(v) Which will have the greater entropy, a mole of oxygen gas molecules or a mole of solid copper atoms? Explain your answer in terms of the motion and arrangement of the particles present. [3]

b) An enthalpy level diagram is shown below for the dissolving of anhydrous copper(II) sulphate in water.

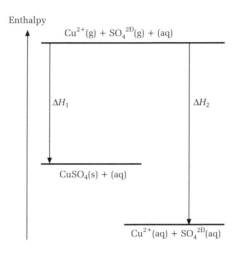

(i) Choose terms from the following list to describe the enthalpy changes indicated by ΔH_1 and ΔH_2 in the diagram:

enthalpy of activation	hydration enthalpy
bond enthalpy	enthalpy change of ionisation
enthalpy change of formation	lattice enthalpy

[2]

(ii) Draw an arrow on a copy of the diagram above to represent the enthalpy change of solution (ΔH_{soln}) of $CuSO_4(s)$. [1]

(iii) Would you expect the temperature of the water to rise or fall when anhydrous copper(II) sulphate dissolves? Explain your answer. [2]

(iv) In copper sulphate solution, the ions are said to be **hydrated**. Draw a labelled diagram of a hydrated copper(II) ion to show what this means. [3]

[O & C (Salters), specimen]

Answer	Comment

Answer

a) (i) [a copper atom]
$$1s^2 2s^2 2p^6 3s^2 3p^6 3d^{10} 4s^1$$
[a Cu^{2+} ion]
$$1s^2 2s^2 2p^6 3s^2 3p^6 3d^9$$

Comment

Cu^{2+} is transitional as it has a part full d shell.

(ii)
iron	[oxidised]	+2	+3
sulphur	[oxidised]	−2	+4

Oxidation numbers are more often written in Roman numerals.

Remember the sum of the oxidation numbers of the atoms in a neutral compound is equal to zero. Uncombined elements have an oxidation number of zero.

(iii) $M_r(CuFeS_2) = 64 + 56 + (2 \times 32) = 184$

This contains $\dfrac{64}{184}$ copper by mass.

The rock contains $\dfrac{0.50}{100}$ of chalcopyrite.

So the percentage of copper in the rock is

$$\frac{64}{184} \times \frac{0.50}{100} \times 100\% = 0.17\%$$

Don't give more than two significant figures in your final answer because the numbers you are working from have two significant figures, so this is the limit of accuracy.

Trouble with the maths?

When you are asked for the percentage present and you don't quite know how to begin, it may help with the maths if you find out how much is present in 100 g (which will give you the same numerical answer) and do all your working in grams. In this case, we know that 100 g of rock contains 0.50 g of chalcopyrite (and indeed 100 tonnes would contain 0.50 tonnes, 100 lb would contain 0.50 lb, etc.) because that is what 0.50% means. Your problem then becomes how to find the mass in grams of copper in 0.50 g of $CuFeS_2$.

You know that any mass of it contains the fraction $\dfrac{64}{184}$ copper (see above).

So 0.50 g contains $\dfrac{64}{184} \times 0.50$ g $= 0.17$ g

If you can't work out the logic of this, then use $M_r(CuFeS_2)(64 + 56 + (2 \times 32))$ is 184, so 184 g contains 64 g of copper.

1 g contains $\dfrac{64}{184}$ g of copper.

So 0.50 g contains $\dfrac{64}{184} \times 0.50$ g $= 0.17$ g

100 g of chalcopyrite therefore contains 0.17 g of copper $= 0.17\%$.

(iv) There will be large amounts of waste rock to be disposed of, which would either be an eyesore or require costly transportation and disposal.

(v) The oxygen, which has the greater disorder: gaseous oxygen molecules are in rapid motion and are randomly arranged whereas copper atoms are not free to move and have an ordered arrangement.

Remember: entropy is degree of disorder.

b)

(i) ΔH_1: lattice enthalpy

Also called lattice energy.

ΔH_2: hydration enthalpy

Also called hydration energy.

(ii)

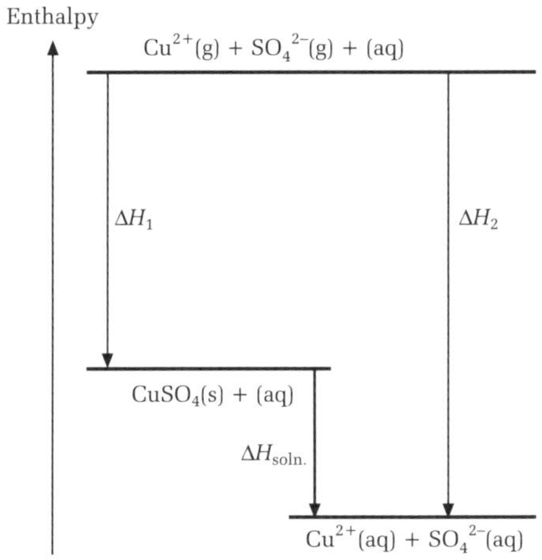

Enthalpy

$Cu^{2+}(g) + SO_4^{2-}(g) + (aq)$

ΔH_1

ΔH_2

$CuSO_4(s) + (aq)$

$\Delta H_{soln.}$

$Cu^{2+}(aq) + SO_4^{2-}(aq)$

The arrow goes *from* solid copper sulphate *to* the separate ions in solution.

(iii) Rise: the diagram shows that heat is given out in this process, so this will heat up the solution.

It is an exothermic reaction.

(iv)

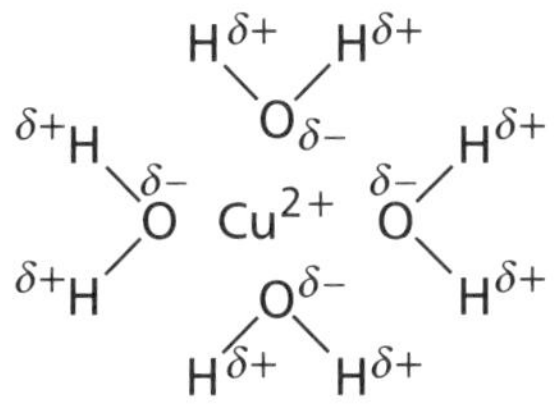

$H^{\delta+}$ $H^{\delta+}$

$^{\delta+}H$ $O_{\delta-}$ $H^{\delta+}$

$^{\delta-}O$ Cu^{2+} $O^{\delta-}$

$^{\delta+}H$ $O_{\delta-}$ $H^{\delta+}$

$H^{\delta+}$ $H^{\delta+}$

It is not certain exactly how many water molecules surround the Cu^{2+} ion. Drawing four makes the point. You need to show the charge on the copper ion, the dipoles on the water molecules and that the $O^{\delta-}$'s are attracted to the Cu^{2+}.

2 The theme of this question is elements of Group IV and their compounds.

It tests:

- your understanding of bonding and its relationship to properties (Chapter 9)
- your understanding of intermolecular forces (Chapter 10)
- your understanding of equilibrium (Chapters 11 and 23)
- your understanding of environmental chemistry; the greenhouse effect (Chapter 27)

Carbon dioxide is used to add the 'fizz' to fizzy drinks. It is dissolved in water under pressure and when the pressure is released the 'fizz' appears.

a) Carbon dioxide molecules contain covalent bonds. Explain what you understand by the term **covalent bond**. [2]

b) (i) On the molecule of carbon dioxide drawn below, indicate which atom(s) is/are positively polarised and which negatively polarised.

$$O=C=O$$ [1]

(ii) Explain why carbon dioxide has no overall dipole. [2]

(iii) Name the type of bonding found **between molecules** in carbon dioxide. [1]

c) In a stoppered bottle of fizzy drink, the following chemical equilibrium exists:

$$CO_2(g) \rightleftharpoons CO_2(aq)$$

(i) Chemical equilibria are sometimes described as dynamic equilibria. Draw a labelled diagram of the surface of the solution in a stoppered bottle of fizzy drink and use it to illustrate what you understand by the term **dynamic equilibrium** for the reaction in the above equation. [3]

(ii) When the stopper is removed from a bottle of fizzy drink it goes 'flat' because much of the dissolved carbon dioxide comes out of solution. Use your understanding of chemical equilibrium to explain why this happens. [3]

d) The concentration of carbon dioxide in the atmosphere is gradually increasing. There are concerns that this will enhance the 'greenhouse effect' and contribute to global warning Draw a labelled diagram to explain the **greenhouse effect** in the Earth's atmosphere.

[5]

e) Silicon is in the same group of the Periodic Table as carbon, yet its oxide, SiO_2, is a giant covalent structure, with each silicon atom covalently bonded to four oxygen atoms and each oxygen atom covalently bonded to two silicon atoms.

(i) Draw a diagram to illustrate this structure which shows the 3-dimensional arrangement of bonds around the silicon atom. [2]

(ii) State and explain a physical property of silicon dioxide which results from this structure. [2]

[O & C (Salters), specimen]

Answer

a) A bond in which a pair of atoms is held together by sharing a pair of electrons.

b) (i)
$$\overset{\delta-}{O}=\overset{\delta+}{C}=\overset{\delta-}{O}$$

(ii) The molecules are linear and the dipoles cancel out.

(iii) Dipole–dipole

c) (i)

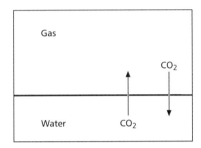

At equilibrium, carbon dioxide molecules move out of the water and into it *at the same rate*, so the concentrations of carbon dioxide in each phase do not change.

(ii) $CO_2(g)$ molecules will now escape from the bottle at a greater rate than they will redissolve, so the concentration of $CO_2(aq)$ drops.

d)

High frequency ultraviolet and visible radiation from the Sun passes through the atmosphere

Lower frequency infra-red radiation is radiated out

Troposphere

EARTH   Atmosphere

The lower frequency radiation is trapped by gases (including CO_2) in the atmosphere and heat builds up.

Comment

Oxygen is $\delta-$ because it is more electronegative than carbon.

In a non-linear molecule such as water,

$$\overset{\delta-}{\underset{\underset{\delta+\,H \qquad H\,\delta-}{}}{O}}$$

the two dipoles do not cancel and the molecule has an overall dipole.

van der Waals forces might also be acceptable because these forces operate between *all* molecules, but dipole–dipole forces are stronger.

There are three marks for this question, so try to make three points. You could also explain this by reference to Le Châtelier's principle: when the bottle is opened the concentration (or pressure) of $CO_2(g)$ drops, so the equilibrium $CO_2(g) \rightleftharpoons CO_2(aq)$ is driven left to counteract the change. This means there will be less $CO_2(g)$ above the liquid surface and CO_2 molecules will escape from the liquid.

Again there are five marks for this question so the perfect answer should have five points. Remember lower frequency (infra-red radiation) has a longer wavelength. You should show this clearly in your diagram. The troposphere is the region of the Earth's atmosphere which is closest to the surface – extending to about 20 km altitude. Above it is the stratosphere.

e) (i)

The oxygen atoms are arranged tetrahedrally around the silicon atom. Use wedge and dotted bonds to show the three-dimensional nature.

(ii) Silicon dioxide has a very high melting point because it has a giant structure with a network of strong covalent bonds which require a lot of energy to break.

You could alternatively say it was a solid or hard because of the regular pattern and rigidity of a giant covalent structure.

3 The theme of this question is finding the structure of an organic acid.

It tests:

- Your ability to plot and interpret graphs (Chapter 6)
- Your ability to do simple chemical calculations (Chapter 4)
- Your recall of the meaning of the term 'end point'
- Your ability to recall and use the equation
  $pH = -\log_{10}[H^+]$

and $K_a = \dfrac{[H^+(aq)]_{eqm}[A^-(aq)]_{eqm}}{[HA(aq)]_{eqm}}$

(Chapters 12 and 24)

- Your ability to interpret mass spectra (Chapters 29 and 38)

A carboxylic acid **A** contains 40.0% carbon, 6.70% hydrogen and 53.3% oxygen by mass. When 10.0 cm^3 of an aqueous solution of **A**, containing 7.20 g dm^{-3}, was titrated against 0.050 mol dm^{-3} sodium hydroxide, the following pH reading were obtained.

Volume NaOH/cm^3	0.0	2.5	5.0	7.5	10.0	14.0	15.0	16.0	17.5	20.0	22.5
pH	2.5	3.2	3.5	3.8	4.1	4.7	5.2	9.1	11.5	11.8	12.0

a) (i) Plot a graph of pH (on the y axis) against volume of NaOH (on the x axis). Use the graph to determine the end point of the titration. Hence calculate the relative molecular mass of **A**. [8]

(ii) Calculate the value of K_a for **A** and state its units. [4]

b) Calculate the molecular formula of **A**. Given that **A** contains one asymmetric carbon atom, deduce its structure. Briefly indicate your reasoning. [4]

c) The mass spectrum of **A** show major peaks at m/e values of 15, 30, 45 and 75. Suggest a formula for the species responsible for each of these four peaks [4]

d) Describe a series of tests you would perform in order to confirm the structure obtained in (b), given that you already know that it is an acid. [5]

Answer

a) i)

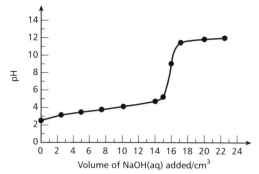

Graph of pH against volume of base added to acid **A**

The end point is approximately 15.8 cm^3 of NaOH.

At the end point:

$$\text{Number of moles of NaOH} = \frac{0.050 \times 15.8}{1000}$$

$$= 7.9 \times 10^{-4} \text{ mol}$$

$$RCO_2H(aq) + NaOH(aq) \longrightarrow$$
$$RCO_2Na(aq) + H_2O(aq)$$

Assuming the acid is monoprotic, there will be the same number of moles of acid **A** as sodium hydroxide in the reaction.

So, 10 cm^3 of acid **A** contains 7.9×10^{-4} moles and therefore 1000 cm^3 (1 dm^3) contains $7.9 \times 10^{-4} \times 10^2$ moles $= 7.9 \times 10^{-2}$ moles.

We know that the concentration of the acid is 7.20 g dm^{-3}.

So, 7.9×10^{-2} mol of acid **A** has a mass of 7.20 g and 1 mole of acid **A** has a mass of

$$\frac{7.2}{7.9 \times 10^{-2}} \text{ g} = 91.1 \text{ g}$$

Therefore M_r of acid **A** = 91 (to 2 s.f.)

Comments

Don't forget to label the axes with the quantity you are plotting and units if appropriate. (Remember pH has no units). You should also include a title.

The end point is the volume of sodium hydroxide that has been added when the pH rises steeply. If you were using an indicator for the titration you would have to select one that changed in the near-vertical portion of the pH curve. Note that the pH at the end point is not exactly 7 (neutral). This is a titration of a weak acid with a strong base and hydrolysis of the salt formed will make the pH slightly alkaline at the equivalence point – the point at which the same number of moles of acid and base are present in the solution.

The salt is RCO_2Na, which hydrolyses:

$$RCO_2Na + H_2O \rightleftharpoons RCO_2H + Na^+OH^-$$

The OH^- ions make the solution alkaline at the end point.

The number of moles of solute present in a solution of volume V cm^3 and concentration M mol dm^{-3} is:

$$\frac{M \times V}{1000}$$

Read the question carefully. An easy mistake to make is to assume that 10 cm^3 contains 7.20 g, whereas it is 1 dm^3 that contains 7.20 g.

Remember that relative molecular mass has no units

Give the answer to two significant figures because this is the number to which the data is given.

(ii) The pH of the acid solution (before any NaOH is added) is 2.5.

To find this antilog use the 'Inv log' or '10^x' buttons on your calculator.

$$pH = -\log_{10}[H^+]$$
$$2.5 = -\log_{10}[H^+]$$
$$-2.5 = \log_{10}[H^+]$$
$$[H^+] = 3.16 \times 10^{-3} \text{ mol dm}^{-3}$$

For a weak acid:

$$K_a = \frac{[H^+(aq)]_{eqm}[A^-(aq)]_{eqm}}{[HA(aq)]_{initial} - [H^+(aq)]_{eqm}}$$

$$HA(aq) \rightleftharpoons H^+(aq) + A^-(aq)$$

So $[H^+(aq)]_{eqm} = [A^-(aq)]_{eqm}$
Since the acid is weak,
$[HA(aq)]_{initial} - [H^+(aq)]_{eqm} \approx [HA(aq)]_{initial}$

So $K_a = \dfrac{[H^+(aq)]^2_{eqm}}{[HA(aq)]_{initial}}$

$$K_a = \frac{(3.16 \times 10^{-3} \text{ mol dm}^{-3})^2}{7.9 \times 10^{-2} \text{ mol dm}^{-3}}$$

$$K_a = 1.26 \times 10^{-4} \text{ mol dm}^{-3}$$

Don't forget the units.

b) 100 g of **A** would contain 40 g C, 6.70 g H, 53.3 g O.

Number of moles $C = \dfrac{40}{12} = 3.33$

Number of moles $H = \dfrac{6.7}{1} = 6.70$

Number of moles $O = \dfrac{53.3}{16} = 3.33$

The simplest ratio of C : H : O is therefore 1 : 2 : 1.

The empirical formula is CH_2O.

The empirical formula is the simplest whole number ratio of the elements in a compound.

M_r of the empirical formula is
$12 + (2 \times 1) + 16 = 30$

The molecular formula is the actual numbers of atoms of each element in the molecule.

$M_r = 91$, i.e. approximately 3 times the M_r of the empirical formula.
So, the molecular formula is $C_3H_6O_3$.

Carboxylic acids contain the unit CO_2H, which can only come at the end of a carbon chain.

So the structure must be based on $C-C-CO_2H$ plus 5 hydrogen atoms and 1 oxygen atom.

An asymmetric carbon atom has four different groups bonded to it. This suggests:

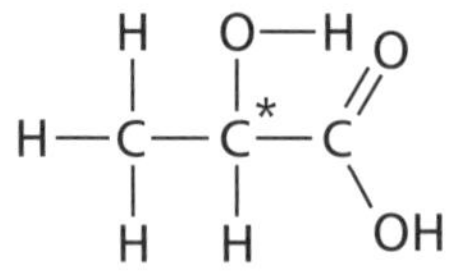

* asymmetric carbon

This is 2-hydroxypropanoic acid (lactic acid).

c) The peaks are probably:

15: CH_3^+

30: $HO-\overset{+}{C}-H$;

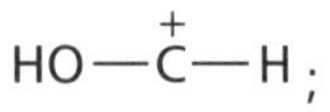

45: or $CH_3-\overset{+}{\underset{H}{C}}-OH$;

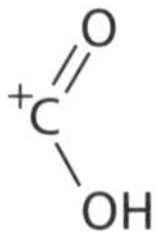

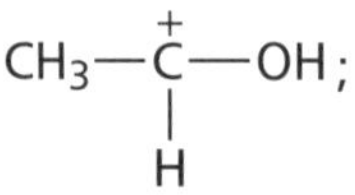

75:

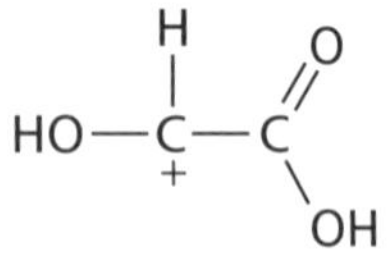

d) Some possibilities are:

High resolution mass spectrometry would check that the molecular formula was correct.

A negative Benedict's test would rule out aldehyde or ketone.

Melting point determination of the pure compound would confirm the structure if it matched that of a named sample.

The infra-red spectrum of the suspected acid would match with one of a known sample.

The triiodomethane reaction indicates CH_3CHOH- or CH_3CO-.

Infra-red spectra would not help to confirm the presence of the —OH group since both —OH and C=O groups will be present from the acid group of the compound.

As there are five marks for the question, try to make five points.

4 The theme of this question is isolating and investigating the structure of an unknown liquid.

It tests your:

- practical experience of chemistry (drawing the apparatus for distillation)
- knowledge of techniques for structure determination (Chapters 7, 29, and 38)
- understanding of hydrogen bonding (Chapter 10)

Some students were investigating butter which had been allowed to 'go off'. They were able to obtain an impure sample of the substance responsible for the unpleasant smell. When they distilled this sample, they obtained a colourless liquid that boiled at around 160 °C. Further investigations showed that this liquid was butanoic acid, C_3H_7COOH.

a) Draw a labelled diagram of the apparatus you would use to carry out a distillation to purify the impure liquid initially obtained by the students and, at the same time, measure its boiling point accurately. [4]

b) Mass spectrometry of the pure liquid helped to confirm its structure.

   (i) Write the following labels (with appropriately drawn lines) on a copy of the diagram of a mass spectrometer shown below:

   sample inserted here;   ionisation occurs here;   electric field;   magnetic field.

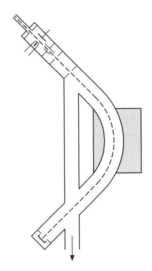

[3]

   (ii) The mass spectrum of butanoic acid is shown below. Indicate which line in the spectrum shows that the substance has an M_r of 88. Explain your choice.

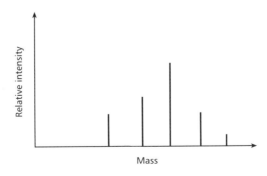

[2]
c) The infra-red spectrum provided further evidence for the structure of the pure liquid and is

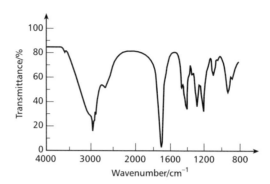

Fig 1 Infra-red spectrum of the pure liquid responsible for the unpleasant smell of butter

shown below in **Figure 1**.
Butanoic acid contains C=O, O—H and C—H bonds. Label on **Figure 1** the absorptions characteristic for these groups. A table of characteristic infra-red absorptions is given on the Data Sheet accompanying this paper. [3]

d) In liquid butanoic acid, the molecules are found in pairs with hydrogen bonds between each pair.

$$C_3H_7-C \overset{O}{\underset{O-H}{}} \qquad \overset{H-O}{\underset{O}{}} C-C_3H_7$$

Indicate on a copy of the diagram below the positions of the hydrogen bonds that would form. Explain, with reference to the bonds you have drawn, the conditions necessary for hydrogen bonds to form. [4]

[O & C Salters specimen]

Answer

a)

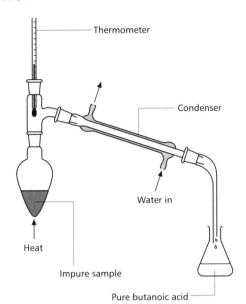

Thermometer

Condenser

Water in

Heat

Impure sample

Pure butanoic acid

Comments

Note that:

- the apparatus should have no leaks;
- the apparatus must not be sealed or it would explode;
- the thermometer bulb must be level with the outlet to the condenser;
- water enters the condenser at the lower connection and leaves at the top (to ensure that the condenser is always full of water).

b) (i)

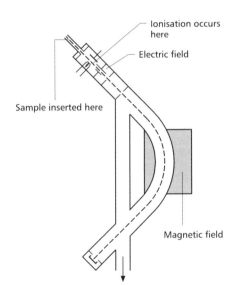

Ionisation occurs here

Electric field

Sample inserted here

Magnetic field

Mass spectrometers vary in shape but the magnetic field is always where the stream of ions is deflected into an arc of a circle.

(ii)

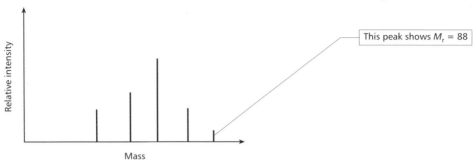

Don't confuse the parent ion peak, of highest mass, i.e. furthest to the right, with the tallest peak.

This peak shows $M_r = 88$

Explanation: This is the peak of highest mass. It is the parent ion and represents the unfragmented molecule.

c)

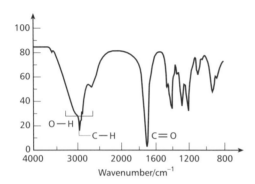

A data sheet would be supplied with the question, but these three IR peaks come up a lot in exam questions and are well worth learning.

d)

$$O \text{ --- } H \text{--} O$$
$$C_3H_7 \text{---} C \qquad\qquad C \text{---} C_3H_7$$
$$O \text{---} H \text{ --- } O$$

Pairs of molecules like this are called dimers. They are formed in pure liquid carboxylic acids (not in aqueous solutions) and make the acids appear to have double their actual relative molecular mass.

Explanation: A hydrogen covalently bonded to an electronegative atom (in this case oxygen) hydrogen bonds to an electronegative atom (again oxygen in this case).

5 Revision and examination skills

Introduction

The best exam tip is to know all your chemistry well! But however much (or little!) you do know, you will do better if you have good exam technique and know what the examiner is looking for.

Revision

The best advice we can offer is make your revision active – it is only too easy to read through your notes without absorbing much content. Some or all of the following might be useful.

- Reorganise your notes.
  Rewrite the important points on file cards.
  Highlight important words or phrases in your notes.
  Make 'spider' diagrams where you draw in links from a central theme.

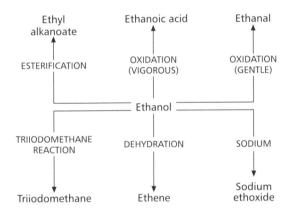

Fig 5.1 A spider diagram for the reactions of ethanol

- Test yourself frequently.
  The summary sections of *New Understanding Chemistry for Advanced Level* have a cover-up system where you can cover up the right-hand side of a sentence and see if you can complete it correctly.
  You can use the official specification (syllabus) for the exam as a basis for your content. The addresses of the Awarding Bodies are on page iv.
- Do as many past exam papers as you possibly can.

Memory aids

A **mnemonic** uses words to aid memory. For example, you might take the first letters of the sentence that you want to remember and make either a new word or a simple, snappy sentence. If you make up a mnemonic try and make it fairly simple, then really fix it into your head. It helps if your word or words have a bizarre quality, or can be pictured.

For example, to remember the order of colours in the rainbow – red, orange, yellow, green, blue, indigo, violet (which is the same as the order of colours in the visible region of the electromagnetic spectrum) – you probably memorise the sentence:

> **R**ichard **o**f **Y**ork **g**ave **b**attle **in** **v**ain (this is how Ted remembers it)
> or, starting from the bottom colour and working upwards, the word **VIBGYOR** (this is how Jan remembers it).

You then could add to this the colour that has the longest wavelength. It is red: shepherds *long* for a red sky at night.

A long(ing) shepherd wants a red sky at night

Fig 5.2 A really bizarre image helps to fix something in your head

Here are some more examples, which might give you some ideas of your own.

- The first four alkanes are methane, ethane, propane, butane

We use **M**onkeys **e**at **p**eanut **b**utter.

Fig 5.3 If you draw your own cartoon of something you want to remember, you will never forget it. It doesn't have to be a masterpiece!

- The three elements that are electronegative enough to form hydrogen bonds are nitrogen, oxygen and fluorine – 'the big three'.

Remember the word 'enough', spelt **ENOF** – **e**lectronegative **n**itrogen, **o**xygen, **f**luorine.

- The CORN law is a way of remembering the spatial arrangement of the groups around the chiral carbon of an L-amino acid.

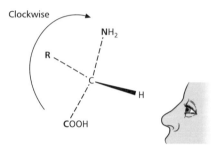

Fig 5.4 Look along the H—C bond and if the groups (going clockwise) are in the order —CO_2H, R— and —NH_2, then the acid is the L-form. If they are in any other order, it is the D-form

- The order of reactivity of metals (the ones in the middle of the list) is magnesium, aluminium, zinc, iron, tin, or **MAZIT**.
- **OIL RIG** stands for **o**xidation **i**s **l**oss and **r**eduction **i**s **g**ain of electrons. This is useful if you need to work out whether an element has been oxidised or reduced when the value of the charge on its ion is changed. For example, in $Fe^{2+} \rightarrow Fe^{3+} + e^-$, Fe^{2+} has lost an electron, so it has been oxidised.
- Oxidation occurs at the anode (**Ooh Aa**h).

Be prepared for the exam

The advice below applies equally to end-of-course exams or module papers.

Make sure you know the style of the papers you will be taking. For example, will the papers be multiple-choice, structured (where you write answers in spaces on the paper) or free response (answers on lined paper)? What content or topics will be examined in a particular paper unit? Will there be a choice of questions? How long will the paper last?

Practice with past papers is important but do make sure you are aware of any changes which have taken place. Each Awarding Body publishes a specification with details of the material you will be expected to know and details of how it will be examined. Some Awarding Bodies have more than one chemistry specification, so make sure you have the right one – check with your teacher.

Read the question

This should go without saying, but do it carefully – especially where you have a choice of questions. It really is worth reading it twice. It is very common to misread a question the first time under the par-

ticular pressure of an exam. Also, you don't want to find out that the question that you thought was about organic chemistry, and leapt into, was really about reaction rates of organic compounds when you've already spent 20 minutes on it.

Time is built into the exam to allow for reading the paper.

Allocate your time

Most exam questions have a gradient of difficulty – that is, they start easily and get harder. So if you are short of time it makes sense to do the first (easy) parts of all the questions rather than struggle to finish just a few.

Know what the examiner means

Examiners have a language of their own and it is worth learning just what they mean by words such as 'state', 'describe' or 'explain'.

Here is a guide to what examiners mean by some commonly used terms.

Define means a formal statement such as 'A catalyst is a substance that alters the rate of a chemical reaction without itself being chemically changed in the process.'

What do you understand by? or **What is meant by?** means that you need to give a definition and some comment on the significance of the term in question. So you might add that a catalyst works by enabling a reaction pathway of lower activation energy.

State means that a short answer is required with no need for explanation. For example, 'The oxidation number of oxygen in water is –II.'

List means give a number (usually specified) of points with no need for explanation. Do not give more points than you are asked for.

Explain requires you to give some reasoning or refer to theory.

Describe means state in words (and, possibly, diagrams) the main points of a topic. If it refers to an experiment, you should say what you would see or the readings you would expect to get.

Discuss implies that you should give a critical account, pointing out pros and cons, for example.

Outline indicates a brief answer covering essential points only.

Predict or **deduce** means that you are expected to produce the answer by making logical connections between other pieces of information – probably ones mentioned (or worked out) earlier in the question.

Comment is open-ended, suggesting that you need to state or work out a number of points of interest and relevance to the context of the question. Exactly how long your comments are will depend on the marks, time and space allocated to that part of the question.

Suggest implies that there is no single 'right' answer. Either there may be several suitable answers or that you are expected to apply general knowledge or chemical reasoning to an unfamiliar situation.

Calculate or **determine** means that a numerical answer is needed. You should show working.

Estimate means give an answer of the right general size possibly by making assumptions or rounding off quantities to simplify a calculation. For example, you might be asked to estimate the fifth ionisation energy of an element having been given the first four.

Sketch, applied to a graph, means that the shape and position of the curve need to be correct but that actual values need not be. However, points such as passing through the origin (or not) are important.

In diagrams, sketch means that a simple, free-hand drawing is acceptable although the relative sizes of parts of an apparatus are important and the diagram should be clear.

This list has been adapted from one produced by the OCR but the words will mean the same whatever the Awarding Body.

Give the examiner what (s)he wants

Look at the space for the answer on a structured paper. This will give you a clue as to how long your answer should be. If there are four lines and you think the answer is 'yes', then think again! Also look at the mark allocations for parts of questions. If there are three marks allocated, the examiner will be looking for three distinct points. If you need more space than is allocated for working out (perhaps because you have made a mistake and had to cross it out and start again), use a sheet of paper. Make sure it is firmly attached to your final script and that it is clear which question it refers to.

Keep the examiner happy

Examiners love signs, units, equations and state symbols. Always include units with your answer where appropriate. But do take care – not all numbers have units. Relative atomic mass and pH, for example, are pure numbers and it is wrong to give them units. Signs are important especially in thermochemistry and electrochemistry. If a ΔH value is positive, put in a + sign. Wherever rele-vant, include balanced equations with state symbols where possible.

Significant figures are significant

Use the appropriate number of significant figures in your answers (see Chapter 1).

Use all the help you can get

In many Advanced level chemistry exams you will be given a copy of the Periodic Table, a Data Sheet or Data Book. There are even some 'open book' exams where you are allowed to take in textbooks. Make sure you know what you are given and how to use it.

You won't get away with...

It is tempting if you don't know the answer to make your writing a little indistinct. The rule here is that if your writing cannot be read and there is a question about what you meant, you won't get the benefit of the doubt.

a) i) Name this polymer

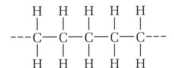

Answer   *Poly (ethane)*

Fig 5.5 Make up your mind. This answer will give you no marks – it is poly(ethene)

It is always better to make a bold guess because then you at least have a 50–50 chance of being right.

On the subject of handwriting – this is expected to be legible. You will certainly lose marks unnec-essarily if the examiner cannot be sure of what you have written. If your handwriting is often not easy to read, then make an effort to slow down, because this can help. Try to express yourself clearly because some marks are awarded for quality of written communication.

6 A-level grade criteria

Grade descriptions

The grade you achieve in your post-16 course in chemistry will have both a written and a practical contribution. There may be up to 30% for coursework. As you might expect, the more you know the more likely you are to get an A, but to help you judge for yourself we have set out an abridged form of the targets you need to set yourself to attain a particular grade. These criteria apply whatever Awarding Body or specification you are following.

Grade A	Grade C	Grade E
Knowledge and understanding You must recall and use knowledge from the whole course with few omissions.	**Knowledge and understanding** You must recall and use knowledge from much of the course.	**Knowledge and understanding** You must recall and use knowledge from some of the course.
Applications You must show a good understanding of principles and apply them in new and familiar contexts. You must be able to carry out calculations even when little guidance is given. You must be able to bring together knowledge from the whole syllabus. *Example*: Be able to write any relevant chemical equation and then use it quantitatively.	**Applications** You must show an understanding of principles and be able to apply them in familiar contexts. You must make some progress in calculations even when little guidance is given. You must be able to bring together knowledge from different areas of some of the syllabus. *Example*: Be able to write the more familiar chemical equations and use them quantitatively.	**Applications** You must be able to apply knowledge and principles in familiar contexts. You must be able to carry out straightforward calculations when some guidance is given. *Example*: Be able to write a chemical equation for very familiar reactions and use a simple equation quantitatively.
Experimental activities You must plan accurately and clearly, use a range of practical techniques skilfully and record your observations accurately. You must then explain and evaluate your results applying appropriate knowledge and using the correct chemical terms.	**Experimental activities** You must formulate a plan, though this may need to be changed, use a range of practical techniques skilfully and record your observations adequately. You must be able to interpret and explain your results but you might need some help in evaluating them.	**Experimental activities** You must formulate a plan, though you may need help to do so. You will be able to carry out the more familiar practical techniques safely and gain results from your experiments. You must be able to explain your results but will need help in applying chemical principles to them.

You may send off to any exam board for a specification and past papers or sample papers. Make sure that these papers apply to the exam you will be taking. They will usually charge a small fee. Do make sure you state the exact specification you are doing. Some Awarding Bodies have more than one chemistry specification. The addresses are given on page iv.

The Periodic Table

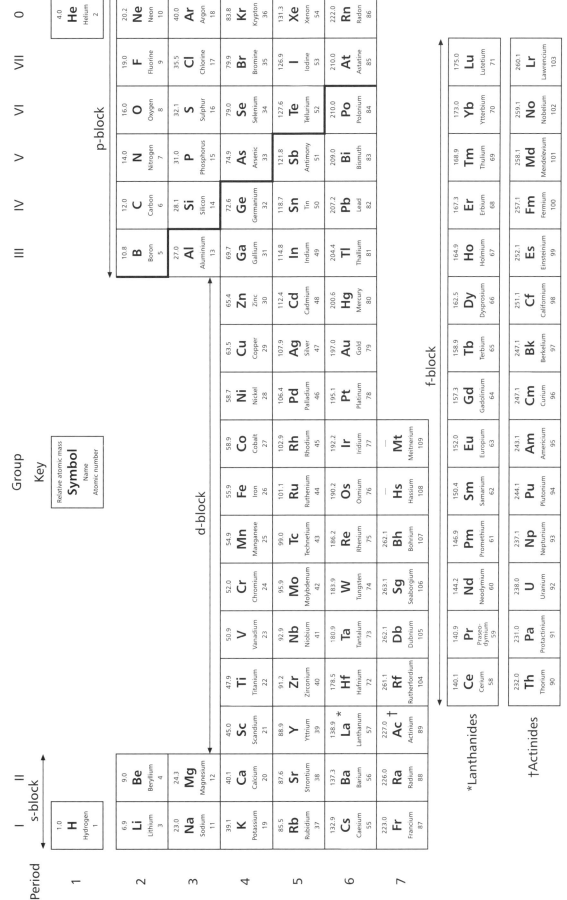

ANGLO-EUROPEAN COLLEGE OF CHIROPRACTIC